MARIA ROMANOV

After 17 July 1918

HALUK ÇAY
Copyright © 2021 (XI) Haluk ÇAY
All rights reserved.
avukathalukcay@gmail.com

ISBN: 9798707144172

"Nobility passes through blood, not by law"
OTMA

Dedicated to my most loved ones
Tuğçe ÇAY & Demir Efe ÇAY

1

Basel, April 1917

Taking the wine glass given by the banker, Kaiser started talking in a reproachful tone, "You lied to me. You said you'd support only me. However, you provide financial support to all sides of the war. My allies are considered as a part of the Holy Roman German Empire. I can understand that you also support the Habsburgs, but how will you explain your lending money to France and England?"

After replacing the wine bottle with no label on it, the banker went across Kaiser and sat down at the table, "I am a banker. I give credit to everyone who meets the appropriate conditions. This is my job. I also do not think that the Ottomans, who are your allies, are attached to the Catholic Church."

"At the end of the war, the Ottoman Empire will be erased from history and become part of the Holy Roman German Empire. But you also help those who oppose the orders of God."

"The God who has chosen you is also the God of his sinful servants. He gives them his blessings, doesn't he?" asked the banker.

"Are you God?"

"God is forgiving."

"You?"

"Never mind me. You accuse me of helping everyone, but you cooperated with the Russian Empire which was your enemy, against the Ottoman Empire which was your ally. On the Caucasian front, are the Ottomans fighting the Russians or the Germans?"

After taking a sip of red wine from the glass in his hand, he continued to look into Kaiser's eyes and talk, "What would German mothers whose children were killed by Russians think about you who was allied with Nicholas in the east? Do your allies know that you want to capture the resources of the Caucasus after the resources of the Middle East?"

Overwhelmed by the banker's questions, Kaiser said, without revealing his feelings, "They will understand that I have made this alliance for the sake of German mothers so that no more German soldiers would die. As for my allies, if you know, they must know also. As the war goes on, you earn more money. You shouldn't be complaining," he replied.

"You're right, but it would be foolish to just hope to make money from the war. For me, one state means one customer, two states mean two customers. All of you will need more credits after the war," the banker replied with a smile.

"Never mind these topics. Have you thought about what I said? Will you help me?"

"Sure," the banker responded. He was also happy with the change of the subject. "Even our man is waiting in the next room right now."

"Who's waiting?" Kaiser asked curiously.

"Do not rush. Let's talk about the terms first."

There was a moment of silence. "I want some pieces of art and jewelry for the cost of the operation. Their names and pictures are on the list," he said and handed an envelope to Kaiser.

Kaiser knew that the banker gave loans against land, especially in times of war. He had a few places in his mind, but he never thought that the banker could demand artwork and jewelry. After opening the envelope and looking at the list, he returned to the banker and said, "What are you planning?"

"Nicholas will be descended from the throne. Goverment will change, and Russia will withdraw from the war. Of course, I will send Alexandra and the children to you as you request."

"So what about Nicholas?"

"The new government will decide his fate."

2

Kaiser knew what this meant. It was clear that the new administration would not allow a former king to live. While these were on his mind, he continued to glance at the list he had. He stared at the list with empty eyes and thought of Nicholas' fate. The banker's words broke the silence.

"Aren't you afraid that Alexandra might be Helen of Troy? You know that the country which she went, had lost the war, not the one that she had come from," he said.

"I can't see Agamemnon around," Kaiser replied, after a brief silence, lifting his head off the list.

The banker could see the arrogance of those who could not pass their passions through the mind filter on Kaiser's face.

After taking another sip from his glass, Kaiser continued, "I did not understand why you need me if you have a man who can descend the Russian Tsar and change the goverment. The man can easily get those on this list to you."

The banker smiled.

"You're right, but you know that I only do business with nobles. The power and wealth obtained in a short period of time blow every peasant's mind. Then he thinks he has achieved success by himself. They are also inadequate in terms of weapons and soldiers."

"What if your man fails?"

"Then we find another one to replace him. A rich and beautiful woman like Russia would be in demand very much."

"Why did you choose this man?"

"He is a good orator with the power to impress people. He is someone who makes people believe that he can save them from their misery. You know, throughout history, human beings have pursued those men who made good promises whether they are true or not. Just like the promise of paradise," the banker replied. But he had not said the real reason for choosing this man, as he thought that Kaiser could oppose. The man who had been chosen by the banker was someone who had sworn to avenge from the Romanov family.

In fact, Kaiser knew that after putting soldiers and weapons into the heart of Russia, he could take the Empress and the children by himself, and then he would not need the banker. However, he knew well that the banker would cooperate with Germany's enemies and cause him to lose the war.

"Okay," said Kaiser, and raised his glass towards the smiling banker.

"Then let's call our friend now," banker said and stood up. But Kaiser asked him to stop by pointing with his hand. Kaiser knew very well who the banker had chosen for this mission. When the banker wanted to meet him in Switzerland, he had understood everything. He also still had a good intelligence service.

"As you said, my friend, I only do business with nobles. My generals will contact the man for details." Kaiser said when he was about to leave the room and added, "Aren't you afraid of the emergence of a new Philippe the fourth?"

On this question, the banker, who began to shake Kaiser's hand more tightly, said, "In order for a new Philippe the fourth to appear, a new Pope Clemens the fifth must appear. You know best that the Vatican is not as strong as before. Most importantly, the period of the fourth Philippe has ended. You have just made a deal because you believed that a peasant could destroy the Russian Empire."

"Yes, we have made a deal. Let's hope everyone keeps their word," said Kaiser and left the room from a door with a sign of throne room on it.

3

The sun was almost about to rise. The throne room of the magnificent castle, located 15 kilometers outside of Basel, decorated with frescoes of ancient Greek gods, hosted its second guest that night.

"We can call you the new Czar of Russia now," the banker said. The man standing in front of the banker smiled. The revolutionary man, who had the facial expression of a wild animal that could jump on his prey at any time, even when he was calm, tried to master his nerves.

"You have a different sense of humor, Baron," he said. The revolutionary man knew that he was very close to his dreams. It was not yet time to give this arrogant man the answer he deserved, which would help him to take revenge from the Romanovs. "I have been fighting against those who suck the blood of my people for centuries. I do not want to be one of them."

"Yes. You are right," said the banker and continued. "You will get the money, weapons, and military support you need" and he handed two envelopes to the revolutionary man.

"It doesn't concern me about your relationship with Czar Nicholas. However, you will ensure that Czar will transfer all its assets that are in banks outside Russia to the foundation, which is written on the paper in this envelope. Also, you will definitely send Empress Alexandra and her children to me. Alive. I will inform you about the place and time," he said and handed a much longer list to the man than the list that he had given to Kaiser.

"I want all the artworks and jewels written on this list completely."

The revolutionary man asked in a low voice without hiding his surprise, "I thought I would send Empress and the children to Kaiser."

"No. You will send them to me. I will send them to Kaiser. This will be much safer."

4

Ipatiev House, Ekaterinburg, 17 July 1918

At 01:00 am, the imperial family was awakened and asked to dress. They thought that the man at the door was the Doctor who came to cure the never-ending pain of Alexei. He told them they were in danger of attack. They would transport the family to another place, and they would take photos in the cellar before they left.

The door of the cellar was closed after the seven members of the Czar's family and four retainers entered in. Soon after this, 10 guards and the doctor came in. There were 22 people inside but there was neither a camera nor a photographer.

The Czarina asked for a chair. "Can't we sit down?" The doctor ordered the man next to him, "Go and get 3 chairs."

Like all members of the family, Maria's suspicions increased. The doctor was lying. When they saw the gun in his hand, they realized that he was not a Doctor, but it was too late for everything. "Rua!" she cried out. "Where are you? If you will come one day, this is the right time."

The person who they thought was a doctor began to speak with a cold and harsh voice,

"Your relations abroad wanted to rescue you. But they are too late. And we are now obliged to shoot you."

Lake Caldaro

5

Tyrol, May 1926

Three years have passed since Otmar was born. Rua's father, Khan, came to the house which he had allocated to me years ago. He had a short chat with Otmar. He gave Otmar the gifts he brought. After a while, we were alone. He said that it was no longer safe for me and my son to stay in Tramin. He said, "The maids can stay with you if you want. I can take them with me if you don't want them to stay with you."

I said, "Let them decide."

He wanted to give me some money, but I didn't accept it.

The next morning, I went to Lake Caldaro with Otmar. First, as always, I visited Rua's grave. I chatted with him for a while. Then we started walking along the lake. The green water of the lake was hitting the beach. The newborn sun behind the mountains was laying its golden lights on the waves. Otmar started to play with the toy he brought with him. I sat on the green lawn. I have started to listen to birds, and watch the flowers. They were my best friends in recent years. Today there was wilt in the color of flowers and a sense of sadness in the sounds of birds. I approached the roses which were turning yellow just like my hopes. At that time, I heard the beautiful voice of a nightingale on my head. I cried while hiding my eyes among the green leafy, twisted flowers, without looking at the bird who wanted to comfort me.

I took a pebble from Rua's grave as a last souvenir. I pressed that little stone on my heart. This stone would be my only consolation on my sorrowful days. I was going to see the face of my beautiful Rua on it. Then maybe I would rejoice by imagining a happy return to Tramin. But the low voice of the wind coming from an unknown place whispered in my ear. "Are you sure?" And it brought unpleasant news from the shores of my homeland.

When I came home in the evening, I read in the newspapers that the last Ottoman Sultan, Sultan Vahdettin, died in the Magnolia Villa in San Remo. "Poor man."

On the following pages, it was written that the body was autopsied and the cause of death was a heart attack. At least he wasn't shot to death just like my family.

The front side of the villa was filled with curious people, as well as with creditors. I thought for a moment that Otmar's father could be there also. I couldn't bear to read more about the sad end of people who were once seen as Gods.

6

The next morning I went to awaken Otmar before the sunrise. I still didn't know what to tell him and how to tell him. "Otmar. Come on, get up." Otmar barely opened his eyes. He looked around with puzzled eyes as if he were trying to figure out where he was.

"Come on, get up. We are going."

"Where?"

Yes. Where? I didn't know the answer to that question either. Maybe we were going to an unforeseen disaster, maybe we were going to the exuberant, troubled days in a foreign country. The maids didn't want to come with us. Actually, they were right. We were going into the unknown. "Don't forget us," they said to Otmar as they both left the house. Together with Khan's driver, four of us would depart. The driver was busy loading our luggage which was consisting of a few suitcases into the car.

"It is time to go," said Khan.

We started walking down the corridor of the house where we had lived for about four years. This wonderful house, hiding the good memories of our happy times in its beautiful heart, was now invaded by silence. The dull light of the moon coming through the windows which overlooked the lake illuminated our path through the flying clouds. The light was following us slowly as if it wanted to increase the fortitude born into our hearts.

Before leaving our beloved home, I looked at the rooms and the corridors for one last time, which were filled with happiness. I reunited with Rua in this house. I gave birth to Otmar in this house. I was going to perform my last duty to our beautiful house, which was containing the memories of this happy life and which ended very quickly like a beautiful dream.

I was trying to comfort Otmar, who was getting cranky. The only consolation in such circumstances was to sleep. But we would no longer be able to sleep in our home.

7

At 5:00 am, they told me that the car was ready. We passed through the magnificent corridors of the house and said goodbye. We got in the car. I thought I saw many imposing shapes in the darkness of the night. It was as if a great object approached us through those shapes, illuminating the terrible night.

The sun was slowly rising. The first lights of the day began to illuminate the houses. The roofs of the houses looked like pale roses. I looked out from the car window. The darkness of the night was wrapped in red lights and the flames of the sun shone on the horizon. I couldn't get enough of watching. Each place was just like a separate poem. We were leaving Tramin. I said goodbye to the city, which looked like a beautiful flower under the light of the sun. "At least you don't forget us", I said.

But among the colors scattered around, even a layer of hope did not fall into my whining heart. I forced Otmar to sleep so that he could relieve the fatigue of the entire night. He put his head on his arm and tried to sleep.

We were passing through semi-dark streets, in front of the houses that were slightly enlightened by the newborn sun. We were headed towards the grieving days of the future. "Our happiness will set with the sun, and the great separation would dry the last drops of joy in our hearts tonight."

We were going through a pretty rough road. Sometimes we entered into a mud mass and sometimes we waited because it was not possible to pass through the pits. The driver could only go on after putting some stones on the road. We took a break by 09:00 am on a lakeside that I did not know. Transparent waves like crystal were banging on the rocks, one or two sailboats marching in the blue waters leaving white lines, and the seagulls were flying away as if they were afraid of our glorious silence. Everywhere was calm and beautiful. A worry-free lake that contrasts with our senses. A cloudless, clear whirling pasture! It was as if the golden colors of the morning filled the sky and the light of the sun spread a glow into the blue water.

I tried to extinguish unhappiness from my heart fluttering like small waves. The clouds flying over the sky were moving by rippling the golden colors of the sun, and two sailboats were breaking away from these blue waters. We continued our disastrous journey.

We finally reached the train station. The spring wind, shaking the leaves of the trees, whispered solace by gently touching our sore eyes. We spent long hours there, wandering around and trying to keep ourselves busy. After a weak dinner, I put Otmar on a bench to sleep. After the tiring day, I needed a lot of rest. I sat next to Otmar and I tried to get some sleep.

8

I woke up at 01:00 am because of the noise. The train was about to arrive. Khan handed out some money with the train tickets from his bag and two passports issued on behalf of other people. I took the tickets and passports and examined them quickly.

Meanwhile, Khan said, "Don't worry. Your passports were issued by the official authorities. You won't have any problems."

They were two French passports with the same names and different surnames. I said I didn't want to take the money. First, he insisted and then he gave up. He kissed Otmar on his cheeks and walked away. Otmar and I were waiting for the train to stop.

"I miss my house. Let's go home. I want to play with my toys."

Otmar's screams drew all the attention. Some people were looking at me with suspicious eyes because they didn't understand what he was saying. Without caring for anyone, I leaned in his ear and said, "We need to be strong. I need you so much."

After that, Otmar never cried again. He stood quietly beside me and took my hand. Soon after we got on the train, we both fell asleep.

We were passing through a forest in the morning. The green trees were calm, the leaves were trembling with excitement and the red flames of the sun were shining in the sky. The exuberant colors that invaded the surrounding area brightened even this dark forest and sprinkled stars on the train windows. I was trying to hear the words of the morning wind which was caressing the leaves.

In the corridor of the dining wagon, children were running and playing games. I told Otmar if he finished his breakfast, he could play also. A few minutes later, Otmar seemed to have forgotten everything. How easy the kids could get along. They all started running down the aisles until they got tired.

A few hours later we were passing by a large lake. The golden lights of the sun were playing with the blue waters of the lake. Among the green forest, there were white houses watching their reflections in the water, as if they had cut off their relationship with everyone. But there was an unforgettable shortcoming and an indelible alienation on these beauties. My eyes were looking for Russia. When I couldn't see her, my eyes were getting wet.

"Oh, my hometown, my hometown," a subtle, elegant voice in the corner of my heart groaned. Another sound was advising to enjoy the lake view as beautiful as the sea, green trees like emeralds, birds with beautiful voices. Then suddenly the previous voice was responding, "Don't you understand the language of the birds? They scream that you are always in exile."

The whisper of the leaves repeated that word. The other voice spoke again and insisted, "Not all you want will be fulfilled."

The other one was crying, "Oh my country, my country." It was like I was split in two. One is a moderate person who thinks of everything with her mind. The other is a delicate, unreasonable, crying child for a broken toy.

9

Our journey continued without any problem until Berig, the Swiss border station in the Simplon tunnel. When the gendarmerie sergeant opened the door for the passport control, I was very alarmed for a moment. I started praying. I held out our passports. The passport officer looked at Otmar for a long time and then he looked at me. I thought he was trying to match the pictures on our passports. Fortunately, there was no problem.

After the great war, the Greek and Austrian Emperors were in neutral Switzerland as refugees. Switzerland had suffered from their political activities. Therefore, they tightened the controls at the borders. Some passengers began to be anxious. Because the train waited at the station in the tunnel for a long time. Some of the passengers were curiously walking around the platform. They were trying to understand what was happening. After realizing that it was a regular check, they boarded the train again and after a while, the train moved again and an hour later we arrived at Lausanne.

The train stopped slowly and we were at the station amongst the powerful electric lamps that illuminated our downcast faces. We went down the stairs with our suitcases. I started to think about how to get to the hotel which Khan mentioned on our way. After asking a few people in the crowd, we met a family who was going to the same hotel. We were very tired and immediately went to the room allocated to us.

10

It has been a week since we arrived in Switzerland and we haven't gone anywhere but the hotel garden. One day we walked on the roads leading to the mountain behind the hotel. Switzerland looked like a beautiful garden. The roads were immaculate, the walls were decorated with flowers scenting around and the green trees were full of birds. After walking for a while, we sat down on one of the wooden benches. We could see the reflection of the big mountain across the lake. It was very similar to our overthrown bliss that we left behind. I looked at large hotels, large streets, elegant houses and I remembered my poor country, which was deprived of this prosperity and happiness. Otmar was looking sad too. Maybe he was thinking about the dark path to the future.

It was time to return to the hotel. The sun was hiding behind the clouds and shining over the blue waters, the snow on the top of the mountains was getting red while we were on our way to our hotel.

11

A few days later we went out again. We boarded a small boat and sailed away, leaving traces on the lake. I envied this happy country. I asked myself, "Why was I thinking about my motherland that did not know the role of mother and threw their children away? Why was I always keeping alive this dream of an indifferent mother in my heart? I remembered my mother's words,

'Russia is our motherland. She is our mother. We should respect her as much as we can.'

But what if she doesn't know her duty to her children?"

I stopped thinking about the past when Otmar hugged me. Otmar was showing me the sunset. After that day we started to go out to walk in the evenings. The days that resembled each other always found us sad and left us sad again.

12

Seven months later, I received a letter from Khan. He was telling that he bought a house for us in Nice, that we should leave Switzerland and go there. He said that exiled members of other dynasties also lived in Nice, that we would be comfortable with Otmar without any attention, and that Nice would be a safer place for both of us. There was no reason not to feel safe in Switzerland. But when I thought that Nice was the place to live the life that my father dreamed of living, I decided to go. I wrote Khan a reply. I told him that I would pay the price of the house, otherwise, I wouldn't go.

I have not had any financial problems because of the jewelry I kept on me since the day I left Russia and the pouch of gold that the old concubine gave me. I had to sell my jewels well below their value at some point, but it was a price to live illegally. I had enough money for the rest of my life.

In the days of captivity, my father told us in which European banks we had deposit accounts and in which of these banks we had safeboxes full of jewelry, the locations of precious metals that were hidden in the mountains, and how we could reach them. Because he was afraid that these would be taken over by other people, he didn't give this information in writing, he repeated it every evening verbally so that we wouldn't forget it, and he made us repeat what we memorized.

My father was an intelligent man, contrary to what many thought. He wanted to guarantee the lives of all of us, as he thought that our future could pass abroad.

After talking about all these bank accounts and safeboxes, he used to say, "The more gold you have in this world, the more money and assets you have. Banknotes, immovables may vanish with a fire. Jewels can become worthless with a small hammer. They could confiscate our assets in banks." After these words, he told us the locations and transportation ways of our secret safeboxes in different countries.

13

Since Khan advised us to leave Switzerland, I thought it would be better to take our gold in this country because we may not have another opportunity. I was able to predict how dangerous this trip would be, but I wanted to go on this journey especially for the future of Otmar.

The next morning, I put the jewels and gold coins in the hotel safe and went to Zürich by train with Otmar. From a shop on Bahnhofstrasse, we bought shoes and clothes suitable for walking in the Alpine mountains during the winter months.

As Otmar grew, he began to enjoy our travels. It was very nice to see new places and to travel constantly for him. I don't know how many of them he will remember, when he grows up. He was constantly asking questions and I was trying to answer as much as possible. I had warned Otmar not to ask questions about where to go next time and not to talk about it with anyone.

14

We stayed at Hotel Central in Zürich that day. The next morning we left the hotel. At around eight o'clock after a long journey by train, we got on various vehicles and finally arrived at the Albula pass. We entered the pension, which was resembling a simple hut at the top of the pass. It was a small pension with two bedrooms downstairs and three bedrooms upstairs. The woman in her fifties, serving tea, spoke to us in French. The tall, old man who came a little later was speaking in Swiss German language.

The man and woman were husband and wife, who owned the pension. The man was from Bern and the woman was from Valais. So the man was from the German-Swiss and the woman from French-Swiss. It was quite surprising for them that I came with a little boy at one of the coldest times of the year. Mr. and Mrs. Schwab gave one of the upstairs rooms without even asking how many days I wanted to stay. It was a village house in the Alpine mountains, with carving boards, feather beds, and old furniture. It had a magnificent view.

When we woke up in the morning, the Alpine mountains were under our feet. We could see until Engadin. I thought heaven should be such a place. When we went down to the breakfast room, I saw that Mr. Schwab was talking to two young girls. After a while, he came to our table. He asked how our first night passed and whether we liked the breakfast menu. Upon answering both questions positively, he turned to Otmar. He asked his name. Otmar did not say a word because I had warned him very seriously about this issue before. Although the man was very surprised, he did not insist. I said, "Our trip was very tiresome. A few hours later, he will talk as much as you want." I tried to propitiate him.

Mr. Schwab pointed the girls and said, "Two girls come here every year from the Teacher-High School to help us. When those who came this year said they wanted to leave suddenly the night before and we called new ones. They can make mistakes during their inexperienced period. If there is a problem, please forward it to me or my wife."

After a while, he brought both girls and introduced them to us. Their names were Maja and Rita. Rita was a long-haired, blond, and very cold girl. Maja was a very beautiful and warm-blooded girl with black hair, white skin, green eyes. We met and chatted for a while. Although Rita quickly left us, Maja chatted with Otmar for a while. Seeing that Otmar, who did not answer him a word, answered every question of Maja, Mr. Schwab said with a laugh, "He will be very flirtatious." Rita looked like a real Germanic goddess. Cold and distant. Maja was a complete Mediterranean girl.

After breakfast, we went upstairs to our room and got the necessary things. We walked from our hostel at Albula pass to the top of Gualdauna. After a little rest there, we came to the Pischa valley. A little ahead of the valley, Kesch Hill was rising. There was an Alpine hut at its foot. I thought we would go there and rest. However, as we were walking on the plain between Pischa and Kesch Hill, we saw a fifty-year-old man with long hair and a long beard sitting on a large stone. In fact, at first glance, the man was looking like a piece of rock. Only when I looked carefully at the man a second time, I noticed the man.

15

I had learned to protect myself in the past years, but in these desolate mountains, I didn't know what I could do with Otmar. As we passed, the man looked neither to our side nor showed the slightest sign of life. He just looked as if he was frozen. Since I was uneasy from the man, we went back to the hostel without going further.

When I entered the restaurant section, I saw that Mr. Schwab had prepared a very nice table. When I asked why, he said, "An old friend's birthday. We were prepared for him. We will have a small party after the meal, and you are invited too."

Then I asked him about the man who was sitting on the rock. "Mountaineers and geologists travel around here. It must be one of them. Don't worry, it's safe here." I was amazed that he didn't ask me why I was here in this mountain at this time of the year and what I was looking for. I thought maybe he didn't want to bother his guests with questions.

When we got down to dinner, we saw Mr. Schwab's guest. His name was Karl Benedict and it was his 70th birthday. He was someone who looked much younger. He was very active, stylishly dressed, and knew how to be the center of attention. Mr. Schwab said that Mr. Benedict was someone who had devoted his life to women, wine, and music.

16

We had our breakfast early the next morning and set off again. This time we did not see anyone around. The weather was cloudless but very windy. Maybe it was much better for us to climb today, I thought. When we arrived at Kesch Hill, we sat down to rest. The view was magnificent. Engadin was lying under our feet.

I started looking for the signs my father had told. This work took a lot of time because the rocks were covered with snow. Otmar was getting hungry. I gave a few pieces of bread and cheese that I brought with me to Otmar. I don't know why at that moment, but I thought we were being watched. I asked myself, what would someone who saw us think about? A woman with a small child was cleaning the snow on the rocks and looking for something.

Finally, following the signs that my father had told, I found the small crescent-shaped plain. After a few steps, I put my hand on the rock that I was looking for. Yes, that was it. In fact, this was not a rock. It was a very well camouflaged door. Although the weather was very cold, there was not a single cloud in the sky. I listened to the sound of the wind for a while. I looked at Otmar's face. He was trying to recognize and understand his surroundings. My inner voice said, "Not today." We went back to the pension.

When we returned that evening, no one was left in the pension except Mr. and Mrs. Schwab and Maja and Rita. Maja loved to chat and play games with Otmar. Otmar liked her too. It was obvious that Maja would be a good teacher. On the contrary, Rita was quite cold. She said only good morning and good evening. Other times, unless necessary, she wasn't speaking at all.

Maja was the child of a mother and father who were also teachers. She was living in Vicosoprano. A deep, huge valley on the southern slope of the Alps. It had a magnificent and unique view. I thought that man wouldn't age there. It was very close to St.Moritz. I was seeing myself in Maja. She was a cheerful, friendly, and a beautiful girl who could easily communicate with people. I hoped her future would be as beautiful as she was.

17

"Are you sure this is it?" Karl Benedict asked the man in his fifties, with long hair and a long beard who was facing him.

"Yes, I am sure. I saw it with my eyes. I even made signs myself after they had left."

"Okay, let's dig into it"

After a few hours, the two old men came face to face with gold nuggets that they could not even dream of. Neither of them could believe what they saw. Ivan, in his fifties, spoke without taking his eyes apart from the gold nuggets.

"I knew Switzerland was a country of vaults, but I wasn't expecting that much. Now how will we carry them without anyone seeing us?"

"Don't worry, man. I thought of it all," answered Karl.

Until dawn, Ivan and Karl carried tons of gold nuggets with sleds down the mountain and then loaded them into Karl's truck. Switzerland was a small country, and the Albula pass was also a very small town. In a very short time, the presence of a young boy and a young woman who came to the pension was heard in town. From that day on, Ivan had started to follow the woman. He thought he received the reward, which was the award of waiting for days in the cold hills of the mountains.

18

On the morning of the third day at the hostel, I went to the hills again after breakfast with Otmar. When we arrived, I saw that the door was open and the inside of the cave was also emptied. I went inside after checking around. I was glad that I was not mistaken in my feelings. Someone was spying on us. But I was also scared. Because when the men realized that what they stole were brass plated wolfram ingots, they would definitely come back. I found the plate, which was the only gold object in this cave that I had to take before I left. Everything was in its place as my father had described. It was a hand-sized gold plate with 117 numbers in 6 rows. With this plate, I would be able to transfer all our gold in Switzerland to anywhere I wanted.

When we arrived at the hostel, I said to Mr. Schwab that we wanted to leave.

"I hope we were able to host you well. I'm taking out your account immediately."

"Everything was perfect. We traveled around. I want to come back at a time when the weather is better," I replied.

We went to our room to gather our belongings. Maja and Rita arrived soon. I thought they stopped by to get a tip. Rita said she would wait outside the door and went out. Maja first greeted Otmar and kissed his cheeks.

"I loved you so much, Otmar. I hope we will meet again someday." She turned to me and said, "A car that Khan sent for you will be waiting at the Preda train station. The driver's name is Adler. He sits in the cafe of the station every day and reads the newspaper of the previous day. Don't worry, the car won't go anywhere until you get on it."

I was so surprised. "You must be confusing me with someone. I don't know anybody named Khan."

"Don't worry, Princess. We know you. Khan has been following you since you left the hotel. He wants to know that you're okay." I wasn't sure if she was telling the truth. I had to decide quickly what to do.

Meanwhile, footsteps were heard from outside. Our door was opened loudly. Mr. Schwab, Karl Benedict and the man sitting on the rock, whose name I later learned was Ivan, came in. Ivan pointed his gun at me. I was asking questions myself. "Where's Rita? Why didn't she warn us?"

19

"Are you going to tell us what you are looking for in these desolate mountains in this cold season?" asked Karl in a very calm tone.

"I don't understand what you're talking about," I replied.

"Let me help you understand then," Ivan said and fired at the ceiling. Years later, I was experiencing the same horror again. In a small and very crowded room, a gun was pointed at my face. Otmar was very scared. He hugged my legs tightly. Maja was standing right next to me. I wanted to hide Otmar behind us, but he persistently wanted to stay with me.

"I will aim for your son next time."

"Stop!"

Everyone turned their heads in the direction where the sound came from. Suddenly silence dominated the room. For that moment I could swear that the room was colder than the peaks of the mountains outside. My body was shaking from head to toe even though I tried not to show. I think we've come to the end of the road this time.

"Haven't you recognized her? The treasure itself is standing in front of you." It was Rita who was speaking. When I looked at Maja, she was very surprised and shocked. She didn't say anything, and she was just looking at Rita. For a moment, I thought that Maja could be with Rita and I brought Otmar closer to myself. I had no idea who was who.

20

"What are you talking about?" Karl angrily shouted.

"That woman is the third daughter of the Romanovs. Maria Romanov."

Everyone in the room was looking at me and Otmar. They were observing every detail of my face.

"What are you talking about?" Karl shouted at Rita.

"I'm not saying anything ridiculous. My grandfather grieved for a long time. There were many pictures collected from newspapers in our house. I can't be wrong. This is her."

Karl came to the bottom of my nose and asked, "Is this true?"

"You all have lost your mind," I replied.

Karl did not know what to do. Rita started talking again, "I'm sure. This is her. I knew it from the first time I saw her."

Karl turned to Ivan and said, "Tie all three." Then he turned to Mr. Schwab, "Apparently, this is our luck day," he said with a smile.

They tied our hands and took us to the corner of the room and forced us to sit on the floor. The three of us were lined up side by side. They went downstairs, leaving Ivan on duty.

"If this woman is really Grand Duchess Maria Romanov, we can't leave her alive. Someone surely will look for us."

"Stop there, Karl. We only negotiated with you about money. There was no murder. Also, I can never let you kill a little boy."

"When we agreed with you, there was neither gold nor a Grand Duchess. I came all the way because of your suspicions. Maybe we couldn't find gold, but as Rita said, we found a much more valuable treasure."

"What treasure? It amazes me that you are believing so easily what a 16-year-old girl has said. Moreover, they will pay for neither the living nor the death of this woman and the child. They will just bring trouble. This is a small place."

"We are talking about the richest family in the world. If this woman is truly Grand Duchess, a fortune must be hidden somewhere in these mountains, which we could not even imagine. If not Grand Duchess, what is this woman looking for in these mountains with a little child in this cold season? Anyone, who knows the location of a hidden cave, should know much more. It is obvious that what we have taken before is deception. There must be more caves that are filled with real gold somewhere nearby."

"I am looking for gold. But I'm not in murder. Promise me. You won't kill anyone."

"Okay my friend, I promise. As soon as you find the gold, everyone will go their own way."

Although Mr. Schwab was not satisfied with Karl's answer, he did not have much to do. He regretted calling Karl, but he could not go back anymore. This blindfolded man was someone who could do anything to get what he wanted. He would try to restrain him as much as possible.

I couldn't understand why they tied Maja with us. But what really surprised me was Rita. If these two girls were sent by Khan, why did Rita reveal our identity? If Ivan was not standing with a gun in his hand, I would like to ask all of them to Maja.

We were just waiting in a corner of a cold room. But what really bothered me was that they also tied Otmar's hands, who had just turned three. Since I saw myself as responsible for the events that Otmar has lived, I could hardly look at his face from my shame. I could only tell him to be calm, that everything would pass.

21

I actually had no idea what our end would be. I was also surprised that Otmar could remain so calm. He didn't say anything, sometimes he was looking at me and sometimes at Maja.

Meanwhile, Ivan said, "If there is anything you know, tell me. I can help you escape from here without telling others." There was no sound from any of us.

The door opened again. This time, together with Karl and Mr. Schwab, Mrs. Schwab came in.

"Untie their hands and make them stand up," Karl said, turning to Ivan.

Mrs. Schwab started to search all of our clothes. After a few minutes, she reached the plate I kept in my waist. She tried to understand what it was first and examined the plate for a long time. Then she turned to those who were waiting there and showed what she found.

As Karl and Mr. Schwab tried to figure out what the plate was, Mrs. Schwab continued to search all the items in the room.

"Are you going to tell me what this is?" Karl asked. I didn't respond. He pulled Otmar by the arm with a stern gesture.

When I made a move to hold Otmar, Ivan put the gun on my head, "Don't take another step!"

"I'm not going to talk too much. Either your son or everything you know," said Karl. It was easily understood from his tone of voice and facial expression that he was someone who could do anything to get what he wanted. Mr. and Mrs. Schwab were looking at Karl carefully instead of looking at us. The screams of Otmar began to echo on the walls of the room. "Mom! Save me!"

"Okay. Leave my son and I'll tell you everything."

"Good. Now you started talking logically."

"First, get us out of this room. We are about to suffocate. If you are going to guarantee the life of my son, myself, and Maja, I will explain to you everything. And you will all live as rich people for the rest of your lives."

We went downstairs, to the restaurant. Mr. Schwab told his wife to check the doors and windows once again. We all sat at a table. Karl put the gold plate on the table. "Let's start with this," he said.

Just as I was going to start talking, gunshots were heard from outside. Everyone at the table panicked. We lay down with Otmar. The windows of the hostel began to break. I could hear someone entering the room.

22

"Everybody lie down on the floor!" someone shouted. Meanwhile, in an agile movement, Ivan took Otmar from my hand and used him as a shield and pointed his gun at the two men who had entered. "Now you guys put your guns on the floor and walk away," he shouted. Then Karl stood up. Mr. and Mrs. Schwab were still lying on the ground. Meanwhile, I showed Maja, who was lying on the floor next to me, the dagger on my leg, and pointed her to be quiet.

Ivan and the two men in front of him were looking at each other while they were pointing their guns at each other. None of them had any intention to step back. One of the guys said, "It's not only two of us. If we don't go out in five minutes, others will come in."

"If you or anyone else tries to make any moves, the child will die," Ivan replied.

"Leave the boy and drop the gun. Get down!" said a quiet voice.

It was Rita who spoke. She was holding her gun against Ivan's back. At the same time, she turned to Karl and said, "You lie down, too!"

It was as if she had done this many times before. She was very cool and confident.

23

"The boy dies!" shouted Ivan. "Be sure, you won't have the opportunity," as soon as she said, Rita pulled the trigger and Ivan fell to the ground with Otmar in his arms. Mr. and Mrs. Schwab were lying on the floor trembling, without raising their heads for a moment. As Rita turned her weapon to Karl, another gun exploded from the left side of the room. Karl fell to the ground, shot in the head.

I got up and immediately took Otmar on my lap. He looked around with dull eyes and did not answer any questions. Then I was in shock for a moment. Time had stopped. I couldn't hear anything. It was as if nobody was moving. Even the smoke emanating from the explosion of guns was not moving.

I came to myself with the scream of Otmar, who was calling me. As I was checking to see if Otmar was okay, I heard footsteps from the left side. The owner of the footsteps told Mr. and Mrs. Schwab to stand up.

"We don't know anything. They threatened us, too," said Mr. Schwab.

"You call this place a guest house, but you have cooperated with the thieves and murderers to rob your guests. You have ignored the lives of women and young children." said the man and fired two shots.

Later, nearly ten more people entered inside the room. I thought they were police officers at first, as all the people who came in were moving in incredible harmony. I thought that we would be arrested and spend the rest of our lives with Otmar in prison or they would kill us.

When I saw that the men entering inside were quickly gathering the corpses and cleaning the floor, I realized that they were not police officers, but this did not cause my unrest to end. Meanwhile, Maja and Rita were trying to help us to get off the ground.

I just couldn't decide what to say to Rita. The girl, whom I thought betrayed us first, calmly saved my son from the hands of that murderer. I still did not understand what was going on. After standing up, I saw Khan in front of me. I was very happy to see him.

24

"I'm glad you're all well. If Rita couldn't call Adler in time, we would be too late for everything," said Khan.

"I told them who you were to save time. I was sure that it would be more interesting than gold," said Rita. I hugged and thanked both Rita and Maja for risking their lives for us.

Soon a few men came over to Khan and said they were ready. Khan turned to me and said, "Come on, we have to leave immediately."

When I looked around, I saw the bodies gathered in the middle of the restaurant. "What about these?" I asked.

"They're the problem of those who will find them. As you can see, they all have guns. Apparently, there has been a dispute between the hostel operators and the customers, resulting in death. Don't worry, we got all the records at the hostel. Your names will not be mentioned anywhere. Your belongings were loaded into the car. Let's be quick," Khan replied.

"We have to go to Zürich first, and then to the Hotel. All our belongings are in the hotel," I said.

"I will take your belongings from the hotel and send them to you. Why do you have to go to Zürich?" Khan asked.

"I have to go to Zürich to finish the job that caused me to come here," I replied.

When we went out, I saw three parked cars in front of the hostel. The men were getting into the cars quickly. Khan led us to the black car which was closest to the exit. The girls also got into the other cars.

I saw lightning flashes and thunder strikes outside and there was heavy rain. I was surprised that I hadn't noticed so much noise inside the restaurant. Thunder strikes one after the other were like flares to show our place. I thought the sky was very angry with us.

25

We were on the road. The road that looked like a river flowing between the high mountains had now really turned into a river, with heavy rain falling down. We were driving very slowly due to the view distance of only one meter. I wanted to get away from here as soon as possible, but apparently, nature hadn't decided yet about allow us to leave.

Otmar had slept with his head on my lap. Since I saw myself as the only responsible person for what happened to him, I was cursing both myself and my fate. If he was born as a child of a family living in those villages I saw, his only concern would be a cup of hot food or his playmates. But Otmar would probably live a chaotic life, and he would never know his real father.

Khan began to speak as if he had heard the words that passed through my mind, "He's a very lucky boy. He has a mother like you. In addition, steel does not become a sword and cut flesh without being burned and being swaged. You can see how calm he can stay in the middle of the chaos. He's a Prince worthy of his ancestors. Do not worry. Only time decides whether the events that happen to us are good or not. He's a great boy and he'll be a good son for you."

After Khan's words, I said to myself, "Well, is this never going to end? Will we always live on the run and always under the threat of death?" Then I closed my eyes to let myself flow through time.

26

"Maria! Wake up Maria"

My dad's smiling eyes were staring at me when I opened my eyes.

"Good morning my daughter. You are lazy again. Come on, all of us are waiting for you," he said with a smile.

When I woke up with a lightning bolt, Khan turned back to me.

"Wake up, Maria. There is a landslide. The road is closed. The police don't allow us to move forward. They may check our identity cards, please stay calm."

I tried to remember where we were for a moment. Although I could not see outside from the window due to heavy rain, I could see that there was a pile of soil and several cars in front of us. According to Khan, there was a landslide down the hill on our left on the Veja Megstra road.

A police officer approached our vehicle soon. He asked who we were, where we came from, and where we were going. Khan said that he was a member of the exiled Crimean Dynasty and that he was with his entourage. The face of the police officer, who was not happy with what he had heard, could clearly be read from his expression. After examining the three cars as much as possible, he asked for everyone's passports.

The police officer examined every passport that he had taken with extreme care. I was holding my breath in every new passport he was examining, and breathing again when he was giving it back. My heartbeat accelerated.

"Are you a French citizen, madame?"
When he asked me, I didn't even know what to say. I couldn't even decide in which language I should answer. Awaiting an answer to his question, the police officer continued to look at me and Otmar with even more suspicious eyes.
After a long silence, "Are you asking me?" I could say.
"Is there any other lady in the car?"
"I'm sorry I didn't understand. Yes, I am a French citizen."
"What is your reason for travel? Are you a dynasty member?"
I was looking at Khan with begging eyes, but because he was in the front seat, he couldn't see me.
"No. We were in Saint Moritz with my son. We missed the train going to Lausanne. At the train station, we met Khan. He showed us the courtesy of taking us to the first available train station."
"What were you doing in Saint Moritz?"

27

I was sure that the police officer knew what had happened at the hostel. Although first I regretted that I was after the gold, this feeling disappeared shortly after. Yes, we could have lived a comfortable life without these gold nuggets, but I also had to think about my son's future. In addition, I had no tolerance of losing my heritage anymore. With the revolution, everything that belonged to my family was confiscated and looted. Finally, they stole the life of my entire family. In the face of the unending questions of the police officer, I thought, 'Apparently, we will continue to live as leaves that are blown in the wind, rather than to root in a place.'

"We wanted to see Saint Moritz. I heard that it was very nice in winter," I replied.

"Where did you stay in Saint Moritz?" he asked.

Under the heavy rain and frequent lightning bolts, inside the raincoat, the tall police officer, whose face was vaguely perceivable, was no different from an executioner.

"We didn't stay anywhere. We went there for a day trip. Since we didn't have a place to stay when we had missed the train, I didn't decline Khan's gentle offer," I said.

I started to think about what would happen if we were all arrested. If Khan and his friends were arrested, there was no one I could safely consign Otmar. I never thought of leaving Otmar, but I never wanted him to live in prison with me. I was praying for Khan to create a miracle and save us again.

"From which city did you go to Saint Moritz? What time did the train leave?" he asked.

Meanwhile, a man dressed in the same raincoat approached to the police officer. As far as I could see, he was also a police officer. He said loudly that a lightning struck and a fire started in the Pension at the Albula Pass. It was easily understood that the police officer who constantly asked me questions was not happy with that news. He was like a hunter who was about to snatch his prey. After a short silence, he said to his friend, "Take these to the police station. Let them take their testimony about the hostel."

Yes, there was no doubt anymore. Police officers knew what had happened at the hostel at the Albula pass.

Although the Albula pass was governed by the canton of Graubünden, they said that they would temporarily take us to the police center in Saint Moritz as the road was closed.

28

I started to think about what could happen if my real identity was revealed. I thought of the newspaper headlines, Russia and the murderers that would follow us. I could not find a satisfactory answer to the question of what would happen to us. Meanwhile, Otmar kissed my cheek and said, "I love you very much, Mom."

I could no longer hold my tears. We hugged each other and started crying.

Khan turned to me with his usual calm manner and said, "Don't worry, they don't know anything. Even if they found the corpses, they had no evidence to blame us. There was not even an eyewitness around. Our men were around everywhere about three hundred meters from the hostel."

Time was passing, but it seemed day and night were mingled due to the heavy rain clouds in the sky. As we were approaching the hostel, we saw very dense fumes rising from far away. When we got to the hostel, the whole convoy stopped with the police car in front.

Two police cars and a fire truck, and about nine police officers and firefighters stood in front of the hostel. There was smoke coming from the roof of the building, and flames were gushing from the windows. The rain prevented the roof from catching fire, but it did not prevent the fire inside of the hostel. Although the noise of the rain suppressed the noise of the fire, it could not prevent the reflection of the temperature. The temperature of the flames was felt even from inside the car.

One of the police officers, who was taking us to Saint Moritz, got out of his car and went near the other police officers. After a short conversation, they all started looking towards our car. After a short while, we continued on our way.

29

We stopped in front of the Saint Mortiz cantonal police station. They took all of us into the station. First, they searched our clothes and put all our belongings in separate baskets. Then they took our photos. They took me, Otmar, Maja and Rita to a separate room, and men to another room. We waited there for a long time without talking. Otmar didn't say a word either.

I turned to Rita and Maja and said, "Thank you for everything you have done. If my son and I are still alive, it is with the help of you. You don't have to endure anymore. I'll take all the blame on me. Do not worry. I will do my best to get you out of here as soon as possible and make you reunite with your families."

"We're already with our family," Maja said. Her answer made me happy and sad at the same time. For years we had been betrayed by our closest relatives. Now, these two young girls that I saw for the first time in my life continued to support me and my son, without ever complaining about their situation.

For about an hour, we waited and sat on a board attached to the wall in a room of two square meters and without a window. Sometimes Maja and Rita were trying to chat with Otmar and make him forget the situation that we were in.

After a while, the door was opened. A middle-aged police officer with a medium height, with white hair appeared on the door. He wanted me to follow him. I looked at Maja and Rita. Maybe we were looking at each other for the last time. I hugged them, after thanking again and again.

"Forgive me for getting you in trouble. I hope you will have your freedom in a short time," I said.

"Don't worry, princess. Khan will surely find a way. We will go out together as we come here." said Maja.

30

After the young girls kissed Otmar, we headed to the door. We were following the police officer along narrow and dim corridors. Since I didn't want to know where we were going, I didn't ask any questions. We were moving without even knowing where we were in the building. We stood in front of the last room on the right of the last corridor we entered. He opened the door with the key which he took out of his pocket. While I was expecting that we would enter a small and dark interrogation room like a cell, we entered a bright well-lit room with simple and beautiful furniture. The police officer pointed at the sofa opposite us and asked us to sit down. He sat down at the desk and took the phone. I thought we should be in his room.

He spoke to someone quietly on the phone and then turned to me and said, "Please wait, I'll be right back. If you want to drink something, you can get whatever you want from the cupboard."

He hadn't locked the door. I thought if they were setting a trap for us. Did they want me to try to escape? I didn't understand what they were trying to do. We continued to sit. Otmar stood up and started looking out of the window. It was dark and nothing was visible other than the lights of the city. When he got tired of looking through the window, he started to wander around the room. Actually, I wanted him to sit next to me, but I didn't want to get involved because he already had things that a little boy shouldn't have experienced.

After sitting in the room for about half an hour, the door opened. The police officer who just walked out of the room came in with a white, long, straight-haired woman in her eighties, walking with difficulty. The old woman was walking slowly with support from the walking stick in her hand. The man sat back at the desk. The woman was walking slowly towards me.

After looking at me carefully for a while, tears began to flow from the woman's eyes. Then she bent to my knees and said, "Grand Duchess Maria! God, thank God." She took my hands in her hands and started kissing them.

When I looked at the police officer to find out what happened, I saw that he was trying to wipe off the tears in his eyes.

"I had prayed for you for days. I never lost hope. I knew you would be saved. Are there any other survivors? Is the Czar alive?" The old woman asked while crying.

31

We were in Switzerland and our murderers had been living in this country before going to Russia. I could swear that this old woman and the police officer had set a trap for me and my son. After holding the old woman's hands and taking them away from me, "Madame, you are making a mistake. I'm not Grand Duchess. I have no idea what you mean."

After these words, the old woman looked at my face for a while, without acting and saying nothing, as if she was disappointed. If the police officer, who brought her to the room, had not come and lifted her, I would have doubted that she was still alive. As the police officer sat in the chair in front of the old woman's desk, she continued to speak, "This is not possible. You are the Grand Duchess. My husband was one of the palace guards. I have seen you closely many times. I can't be wrong!"

On these words of the woman, even though I thought she might be sincere for a moment, I was determined to be cautious. I told the woman again that I was sorry and that I was not a grand duchess.

The police officer seated the old woman on the couch and, after making sure that she did not have any health problems, he came to me with a passport which Khan gave me at the train station. As soon as I started praying that there was no problem with the passport, the man started talking.

"Don't worry your highness! My mother-in-law and her family were loyal servants of your family. The French government gave passports to many exile dynasty members. The serial numbers of these passports are different from those given to French citizens. Your passport number is from these special numbers. Your face was very familiar to me when I first saw you. Even though according to the records you are a French citizen when I saw that your passport number belongs to the members of the exiled dynasty, I notified my mother-in-law, who was the person who would know you best in this life."

My nightmares were coming true. My identity would be exposed and the next day I would be in the headlines of the newspapers. We would never be safe again. Rua was right. A man could not escape his fate. Living as a dead-known person was much better than being a living dead.

"I'm sorry, but I'm not the person you assume. There are certainly logical answers that French authorities can give to your claims about the passport number," I said.

"Four dead bodies were found in the hostel at Albula. Pension managers Mr. and Mrs. Schwab, a man from the locals named Ivan and an old man named Karl Benedict. I don't know why, but together with other people inside, you are all considered as murder suspects. You may be detained until the investigation ends. I can't do anything for others, but if you let me, I might let you and your son escape from here. I can do nothing if you are transferred to the Graubünden police station."

"I have no idea about anything that you're telling. I know nothing about my passport number, murders, or the grand duchess. Moving to Graubünden or somewhere else does not change anything. I think that those who accuse us of committing murder must have serious evidence. I hope there is a logical explanation for our being held here with my son because someone has suspected it."

32

There was a long silence in the room. I could see tears draining from her cheeks. She was looking at me and Otmar with her tired blue eyes.

"What is your name, young man?" she asked Otmar. Despite his young age, Otmar had learned how to live in exile. He wouldn't talk to anyone that he didn't know. He did so again and left the old woman's question unanswered and he hugged me.

At that moment I couldn't hold myself anymore. I stood up and started yelling.

"At least keep away a little kid from your ridiculous claims. I will not talk. Wherever you take me. It will turn out that I am innocent."

The old woman tried to dominate her tears for a while. Then she started to speak, while she was leaning her head forward, "Grand duchess, on your eleventh birthday, you wrote under your white shoes that one day you would fly around the world with those magical shoes. One of the children who saw the writing while playing in the garden started to make fun of you. When your father came and saw you sad and understood the situation, he said, 'My beautiful and smart girl can achieve anything she wants. Would you take me with you on this journey?' My husband, who was in charge of the palace that day, told about this incident. I prayed a lot for you. If you don't believe me now, I'll stop. But as I believe, if you are grand duchess Maria, please let my son help you."

The woman was telling the truth. In fact, my sisters, who saw that the children were making fun of me, had come and comforted me. Olga was angry with those children, and she moved them away from us. The families who were embarrassed by their children's behavior brought the kids one by one to apologize.

Even at that moment, I believed that my shoes could make me fly to wherever I wanted. You have to believe in miracles. Just like Rua saved my life. Remembering those moments, I was trying to hide my tears from those in the room. I had kept those white shoes until the day we were sent from the palace. Who knows where were they now? I hope they made happy a child in need. I hope they took her to her wishes.

"I am very sad. I heard about what happened to the Grand Duchess and her family. I was very sorry for them. But I am not Maria Romanov."

33

The old woman stood up with difficulty and barely bowed on her knees and greeted Maria. Maria smiled and nodded. The police officer took the old woman out of the room. As they moved slowly in the corridor, the woman turned to the police officer,

"She is Grand Duchess Maria Romanov. Help her. This is my last wish from you." The police officer nodded, hoping that no one had heard what the old woman had said. Then he ordered another officer to take Maria and her son next to the other girls and left the building with the old woman.

34

Maja and Rita, who saw Otmar and me, stood up with joy and hugged us both. I did not tell the girls what we lived in the room. Instead, I said that the police officer asked many questions about my identity.

While we were away, they had brought a few pieces of food into the room. Together with Otmar, we ate the leftovers of the girls. As the room we were in had no windows, it was difficult to guess the time. I asked the girls if they had any news from Khan. There was no news. They had not seen anyone else other than the police officer who brought food to the room.

Otmar went to sleep. Then I didn't know when I fell asleep, but when I woke up due to the noise of the iron door's opening, four police officers were standing in front of us. Maja, Rita and Otmar woke up before me and were sitting quietly not to wake me up. One of the officers standing at the door said, "Get ready. We are leaving."

As we moved in line in the corridor, the police officer who took us to his room with the old woman yesterday came to me and handed me a small piece of paper. I didn't know what to do or what to say. After pointing to me with gestures not to speak and to read what was written on paper, he left the corridor.

For the first time since I came here, I saw Khan and his men while getting in the cars that morning. His clothes were a little wrinkled, but he looked very vigorous.

35

On our way to Graubünden, "Good morning Otmar. How are you?" Khan asked.

"Good morning. I'm fine."

Then Khan turned to me and said, "Whatever you told the police officer we met on the road yesterday, you must tell the same things to everybody. They must have given information beforehand. There should be no contradiction in your statement."

"I'll tell if I can remember," I said with a smile.

Khan said, "You are right. But trust me, please. Things will go faster after we arrive in Graubünden."

With the speech of Khan, I remembered the paper that the police officer squeezed into my hand. On our way to Graubünden, this time there was a police officer in every car, so I didn't want to take the paper out of my bag. Although I was very curious about what was written on the paper, I did not want to read it.

36

Many secret notes had come to my father during our bondage days. In some of these notes, they claimed that they were members of the white army, and in others, just as the old woman at the police station said, they were loyal servants of the empire. They usually said that they gathered strength to save us and that our bondage would end soon. They would like my father to give information about the situation of the house we were in and the rooms we were living in.

My father did not answer any notes, except one. However, when he realized that things were getting worse, he wrote a reply to a note in the milk bottle. He wrote everything about the rooms that we were staying in, the positions of the guards in the house, the changing hours of the guards, and the bedroom window that was left open at certain times of the day for ventilation. We never took another note again. Although my father knew that it was a scam, as a last hope he replied, but it seems that our real destiny was the one that took us hostage.

We were approaching the hostel. I wasn't looking at that side of the road in order not to suspect the police officer who was sitting next to me, even though I was very curious about the situation. The view that I saw passing right in front of me was horrible. There was almost nothing left of the hostel. The rain, which was falling with the utmost power, could not prevent the wooden building from becoming ash. It looked as if it had been stacked all over the top, scattered all over, and nothing more than pieces of wood remained.

37

When I arrived at the cantonal police station in Graubünden, I took the paper out of my bag and held it in my palm, as I thought they might confiscate our belongings again. When everyone in the car, including Khan, began to get out of the car, I thought I had to get rid of the paper. I couldn't find a place to throw or hide a small piece of paper. I felt as if they would find it wherever I hid. Finally, I thought of throwing it under the seat that I was sitting, but there were police officers who were looking inside the car. I thought about swallowing it for a moment but then I gave up. I saw a small hole in the back of the seat in front of me. I shielded Otmar to myself and threw the piece of paper through that hole. I was wondering what he had written, but my sense of getting rid of it outweighed.

When we entered, things that I was afraid of didn't happen. They did not confiscate our bags or other belongings. I was so surprised. They called all the men into a room one by one, including Khan. Then, they were taking these men outside the police station. I didn't understand anything. How could they take the men, that they had taken into custody the day before as suspects in a murder, into the garden of the police station? Weren't they afraid of them running away? I panicked for a moment that I would be responsible for all of the crimes.

Soon Khan came next to me with a police officer. It was my turn. Since I entered the police station, I hadn't talked to anyone, including Rita and Maja. Khan sat next to Otmar. He turned to me and said, "I'll wait with him."

When I stood up, Otmar stood up with me and took my hand. I told him to wait with Khan, that I would return in a very short time. "I love you mom," Otmar said, keeping his usual calm manner and holding my hand tight. I tried not to cry. I hugged him tightly. "I love you too, my son. Don't worry, I'll be here soon."

When I entered the room, the police officer sitting behind the desk asked me to sit on the chair. First, he asked if I wanted to speak in French or German. I said, German. It was my mother's language. Then, starting from the police control at the

Albula pass, he asked me to tell what I knew about the corpses they found at the pension. I repeated exactly what I told the police officer who stopped us on the way. When my statement was over, he raised his head from the papers in front of him and said, "Do you have any evidence to prove that you spent the day in Saint Moritz? A bill or anything?"

38

I wasn't expecting such a question, but I knew some things about law. "Don't you have to prove that I wasn't there? So, in a sense, if you believe I'm lying to you, you have to prove it."

After a short silence, the police officer said, "The police station in Saint Moritz worked well. The waiters, who saw that you had dinner at Le Papin Bleu Restaurant, testified. The two people at the train station had confirmed your statement," he said.

"I told you all I knew," I said. The police officer seemed to suspect something, but his desperation could be read through his eyes as he couldn't do anything more.

"Well, please read before you sign your statement. Then you are free to leave," he said.

When I went out, Otmar ran towards me. I took him in my arms and kissed him many times. Khan came to us. "Let's go out and get some air."

As he walked towards the door, he warned me, "Don't talk about anything until we leave here."

After Rita and Maja got out, we got in the cars again.

No one in the car was talking about what we have been through since last night. Everyone acted as if the journey we took yesterday was never interrupted. Suddenly, I remembered the piece of paper that I threw in the seat in front of me. After I put my finger in the hole and moved it a little to the left, I found the paper. I pulled it up slowly.

The first thing that caught my attention was the names and the addresses. Then I started reading.

"Your highness. We understand that you do not trust us because of your situation. However, please note that there are still servants all over the world who are loyal to the Russian Empire and the Romanov dynasty. You are not alone. We cannot describe how happy we are to learn that you have a son. We hope that one day he takes the throne, which he deserves, and brings our magnificent empire back to its feet, which had many victories in history. Your secret will go to the grave with us. Upon learning from the police officers who brought you, I told them that if they wanted to call the police station at Garubünden, we could investigate in Saint Moritz. Upon their positive response, your loyal servants here gave a statement that they saw you in Saint Moritz during the day. Whatever happened at Albula, I believe in the innocence of you and your friends. Your loyal servants, who are always at your service."

I folded the paper and put it in my bag. I couldn't hold my tears. Seeing that I was crying, Otmar hugged me. Khan turned to me and looked for a while, then he turned back without saying anything.

I was crying with happiness because I learned that there were people who were still loving my family and who were trying to help us even when we didn't have power.

39

We arrived at Zürich after a long and tiring journey. We stayed at Hotel Central that night. When we got up early the next morning and came to the breakfast room, I saw Khan. I was surprised that there was no one near him. When I asked, he said he sent everyone to other hotels in order not to attract attention.

"What are you planning to do?" Khan asked.

"To survive," I replied.

"I know you have the talent for this. So would you like to explain what made you go to Albula?"

Even though I hesitated to tell him the truth, there was no one else I could trust. But still, some questions in my mind had to be answered.

"Why are you helping us?"

"To be honest, I was very angry that Rua was involved in your rescue. For a long time, I thought about what I should do. I didn't approve of what my son had done, but he made a promise to you. My son did not deceive anyone, he did not lie. I am just helping him to keep his word."

"Did you kill him?" I had been curious about the answer to this question for years. But I did not dare to ask. It was not easy to ask a father if he had killed his son.

"The penalty for breaking the rules is death. By breaking the rules, you endanger the life of not only yourself but also the whole family. Just like Rua did."

I did not know what to say in reply to this cold and strict answer. But I still couldn't get the answer to my question. I gathered all my courage and asked again.

"Who killed Rua?"

"You will find the answer to this question yourself. You're not ready yet. Why did you go to Albula?" he asked again.

"I needed to go there to find the key of our treasure in Switzerland. It is an assurance. My dear father was always thinking of our future." I replied.

"Did you find it?"

"Yes. I found it. But the vault is near here. On the road to Zug."

"What if they don't deliver it to you. After all, you are someone else now."

"Do not worry. This is a company that does not ask questions and does not want them to be asked. The key I have is enough. But if you want to come with me, I wouldn't say no to that."

"I'll come of course, but if you want, you can go to directly to France. I will take those in the vault and deliver them to you."

"According to my father, it will not be necessary. The company will send the vault to the place we want."

"I hope your father is right. But still I think it's not safe."

"Contrary to what everyone thought, my father was right about everything from the very beginning," I replied.

"How did he lose his throne then?"

"You will find the answer to this question yourself. You're not ready yet." We smiled mutually.

I took two rings out of my bag and handed them to Khan. "If you deliver them to Rita and Maja, I would be very pleased. These rings are not the equivalent of what they did, but I want to give a memory of my gratitude," I said.

"Your kindness and your genorisity will make them very happy," he replied. Then, with his serious expression, "I can go to the company if you want. So your identity will still be a secret. Since it is a company that does not ask questions, it should not be a problem for me to go. Just tell me what to do."

I was undecided about whether to tell. But if he would betray or harm me or my son, he would have already done so. I was also sure that it wasn't money. Khan was already a very rich man. Besides, this was a good opportunity that I could test his reliability perhaps once more. I took the gold plate with 117 digits out of my bag and handed it to Khan. "This is the key. You will open the entrance door with this. Nobody should be around when you get inside. If you wait for 5 minutes, a manager has to come and greet you. Show him the key. Then tell them to send our vault to Nice. He will ask you for the account name. You will say 'Dragon'. That's all," I said.

"How so? Won't we take the contents of the vault?"

"No. It is an unregistered banking system. Security and transportation are entirely in their responsibility. They charge a high amount of fee to the customers at the beginning."

"How do you trust them?"

"I trust them just like I trust you," I said with a smile. The name of the account came from the dragon tattoo on my father's right arm. When we were young, we thought that the tattoo on my father's arm was a scar. Then when we found out that our father had a tattoo, we wanted to have a tattoo too. When my father did not allow us, we started to draw pictures on our bodies with makeup materials. We were giving meanings to our tattoos.

"Ok. You go back to your hotel and immediately leave for Nice. Don't stay in Switzerland anymore. I will inform you," said Khan.

I had one last question in my mind. Before I left, I wanted to learn his answer. Although my father used to tell us not to ask questions that we do not know their answers, but it was clear that I would not learn the answer to this question from the books.

"How did you get us these French passports? The police officer said that they had given passports with special numbers on them to the exiled dynasty members."

"You know, there are hundreds of dynasty members in exile in France. I have added you among them. It was not too difficult. With a few high-level bureaucrats and expensive gifts, you can predict that how easy these things can be done."

40

A month later we left lovely Switzerland and arrived in Nice. Nice was always a sunny, cool, fun city that attracted everyone. What a unique blossom of our spring was on the path of happiness that stretches in an endless way. But that ruthless storm dried it all up. It plucked its thin stems and replaced them with the yellow leaves of autumn. I wondered if a new spring would follow this time in life, as in the seasons.

Our new home was located in the hills of Nice, with many rooms, overlooking the sea in a large garden. In the first few months, we spent our time preparing a nice room for Otmar. Our lives were simple and calm. When the weather warmed up, I started taking Otmar to the sea for swimming. Since we had to hide our real identities, I would be very careful not to have a routine. Every time we went to different beaches, in different bays. My favorite beach was at Cagnes-sur-Mer. There were many painters, poets, and writers. I liked standing around a little bit and listening to their conversation. Nearby places were also very nice cities but I didn't want to take the train. I felt like I was going into exile again if I took the train.

I used to get up early in the morning in Nice and go straight into the bathroom. I would fill the tub with water and pour a green oil that resembles the smell of pine. Everywhere smelled like a forest. I used to lie in the green water in the tub for a long time. It reminded me of the days I spent with Rua. I told Otmar his father died in battle. I still had doubts about telling the truth. I didn't tell him anything about his ancestors. He was too young. But I couldn't decide what to say in the future.

After breakfast, I used to spend time with Otmar in the garden, reading a book. In the afternoon we used to go swimming and sometimes we took long walks on the beach. We used to go to the zoo on Thursdays. But one day we gave up going to the zoo. At the entrance of the zoo, the officials said, "A new section has been opened today. You should visit."

They brought natives from Africa. They built the same African village of reeds and grass. It was full of men, women, and children. The men and women were walking around almost naked, and the French visitors were having fun looking at them as if they were watching wild animals. After that day, we never went to the zoo again.

41

The roof of the villa was covered with glass. Since the light was coming from the hill, it was an ideal place for painting. I turned it into a painting studio. I bought many painting materials for both myself and Otmar. We used to paint all day without going out. I turned the room, which was downstairs into a music room. I was teaching Otmar how to play the piano. I used to drink Turkish coffee in the late afternoons. That was a Harem habit. During the years I was in the harem, I always had Turkish coffee with Gülnihal in the late afternoons. I never forgot to drink a glass of water before coffee.

Otmar had no friends. I was paying particular attention to this, but at the same time, I was upset that he couldn't play with his peers. Next to the Roman ruins at the top of Nice, there was a huge building called 'Garin de Cocconato'. This building was subsequently the Matisse Museum. One day, we went all the way up there during our walk. Many children of Otmar's age were playing games among themselves. I let Otmar go to them because I was sorry he didn't have any friends. The children were not speaking French. They were speaking in the language they called 'Niçois'. It was a mix of French and Italian languages. I heard about this language when I was a kid. It was said to be from the Ligurians, from ancient times. In those years, though, some people still spoke among themselves in the Nicosian language. I was amazed to see Otmar and the children got along, even though they did not speak the same language. It was easy to get along with each other when we all got rid of our identities. Otmar and I used to speak Russian, German, English and sometimes Turkish languages at home. I wanted him to learn many languages.

42

Nice, France, November 1931

The people of Nice witnessed a very colorful event on November 12, 1931. The daughter of the Ottoman Empire's exiled Caliph was married to Azam Cah who was the eldest son of Osman Khan, who was known as the richest man in the world in those years. When Azam Cah's brother Muazzam Cah came to Nice for the wedding, he liked another Ottoman princess. They got married too. The newspapers were filled with photographs of Indian princes who came to Nice to marry.

In those years, Nice was home to many dynasties in exile. Thanks to the news, I learned that the Ottomans were also in Nice. We didn't know much about the outside world, because we lived an isolated life. The Caliph and his family were living in the Carabacel villa. On the day of the wedding, we went to the villa. There was a risk of meeting Otmar's father, but I couldn't overcome my curiosity. Although I didn't think he would remember me even if we saw each other. I was just one of the hundreds of concubines in the harem.

The Indian princes arrived with two large open-top yellow Mercedes cars. Since the royal color was yellow in Hyderabad, they also chose the cars from that color. They adorned cars with flowers. The princes wore tight white trousers underneath and Hind robes stretching down to their knees. They had turban and crest on their heads. They had necklaces made of flowers. Those who gathered around the villa were surprised to see such a view for the first time, but they were delighted at the same time. After the congratulatory chapter in the garden was over, the princes took their women and their entourage and settled in the Hotel Negresco. A few days later they went to India together.

43

It was time for Otmar to start school. But I couldn't decide which school to send him to. I also wanted Otmar to know all kinds of people because our future was uncertain. So I didn't send him to a private school.

In France in April 1936, the Popular Front government was established, and Leon Blum became prime minister. It was said that they were trying to establish a similar administration to socialism. The school of Otmar was filled with communist teachers over time. They kept talking about communism. As if our past was haunting us. I was afraid to go through the same things again. One day, one of the lecturers said, "Children belong to the state, not families. Never forget that. You belong to the state, not to your mother and father."

I was very angry when I heard these words from Otmar. I said, "You're not going to that school anymore. We'll find another school."

I went to school the next day and told the principal that I would not send Otmar to school anymore. Then I enrolled Otmar in a private school called 'Cours Moulin'. It was a beautiful school in a very pleasant garden. Most of the students were foreigners. There were native teachers of all languages. French literature and history teachers were also experienced. There was a physics teacher who was an assistant to a renowned physicist Georges Claude, inventor of neon lights.

44

Over the years, Otmar had grown. I decided to settle in Paris so that Otmar could get a better education. But the night before we left, we had to have a long chat with him.

I took him to the Hotel Negresco. I showed him the chandelier made of 16000 pieces of crystal. It was built in France for our Palace in Moscow. But because of the Bolshevik revolution, we couldn't have it.

We sat at one of the tables under the chandelier for hours. The stars of my father, mother, and siblings were falling on me. I could see their faces in the shining crystals. I tried not to show Otmar that I was crying.

Otmar stood up and walked towards the chandelier. He was examining the crystals. It seemed as if my father was lighting up his grandson.

It was magnificent! I admired those blending hues of light, passing from reddish-blue to bright yellow by imperceptible shades.

Then I took him to our church. Many of Nice's early visitors were Russians, and the city's Russian Orthodox Church claimed to be the finest.

Five hundred rich Russian families used to spend their winter holidays in Nice. They needed a worthy orthodox house of worship. My father, Czar Nicholas the second gave this church to the Russian community in 1912.

The interior was filled with icons and candles. The icon wall divided the temporal world of worshippers from the spiritual world behind it. The angel with red boots and wings was the protector of us. Russia's ruling Romanov family.

I decided to tell the truth to Otmar.

"You're a descendant of Kings. You're not like everyone else. You have duties. Our duties come first. Being a prince is a profession in itself. You will not cry. You will not show weakness. It's a shame to show weakness. You'll never show anyone you're upset. You won't laugh out loud. You always have to be sober and staid. You will never leave honesty. You won't just think about yourself. You'll be generous."

45

Yıldız Palace, Istanbul, May 1919

"What is harem?" Upon this question of the newly arrived concubine, the woman slightly above the middle age paused for a while. Because she didn't know if she was asking for an innocent purpose or was she just asking to start a conversation? Then she laughed out loud and, "You don't know where you came? Where have you lived before?" she asked. Seeing the young girl's face flushed slightly and shy eyes, she believed her innocence and began to tell. "The harem is the paradise of some, the hell of many."

Then she hesitated. She suspected that the other concubines sent this girl to make fun of her. She started asking questions to get to know her better.

"What's your name?"

"Maria," the young girl said. She was surprised that those who brought her to Istanbul did not change her name despite the strict admonitions about not talking to anyone about her past. But maybe they thought it was a very common name and they didn't want to change it so that she could answer without hesitation when asked.

The concubine continued to ask questions with curious eyes while staring at the young girl in front of her. "You must have just arrived since they haven't given you a Turkish name yet. When and from where did you come to Harem?"

"They brought me here this morning."

The old concubine began to get angry at the girl's short answers.

"Talk to me! Should I ask from the beginning every time? Who are you? Where did you come from and when? How old are you? It seems that you don't have a virtue since they sent you here to the laundry. Don't make me angry, if you want to work here without any problems. It will not be good for you."

Maria didn't care about her threat. She hardly understood what she was saying. Her Turkish was not very well. As much as she has learned in six months. No one was left behind from her family. She was constantly switching between committing suicide and getting revenge. If it weren't against her belief, maybe she would have already committed suicide.

The old woman kept on talking. "Don't you understand what I'm saying? Where are you from?"

"They brought me here from Crimea. But I don't know where I'm from," said Maria. The old woman smiled and asked in Russian, "Are you a Circassian?"

"I don't know," answered Maria in the same language. The old concubine laughed out loud. "It looks like, we're gonna have to deal with you a lot. I'm a Circassian. Most of the girls here are like that."

Maria was surprised and afraid that if anyone would know her in Harem. Maria began to explain more calmly and comfortably.

"I was a housekeeper in the home of an Aristocratic family in the Crimea. I had been there as long as I could remember. I never knew my mother and my father. They said that they died in a battle. I don't know if I have brothers or sisters. One day, the house was raided, they killed the owners, they put all the servants like me on a ship and brought us to Istanbul. We didn't even know where we were at first. We found ourselves in a slave market. One day a man bought me and another girl and took us to Mehmet Pasha's house. I stayed there for a while. Then Pasha gave me as a present to the Sultan. That's all my story."

Although Maria felt the comfort of being able to tell the story with the same as she was taught, she was worried about the reaction of the old concubine. Did she believe her?

"You don't have a different story. It's almost the same as all the girls here. Didn't you find out what the harem was in Pasha's house?"

It was an allusive question. In other words, Pasha or his son should have taught her what the harem was. In fact, younger girls were generally preferred for this job. Maria was looking old to be a favorite concubine.

"How old are you?" the old concubine asked.

"Nineteen," she said.

"Nineteen? You look much older. And you don't look like a maid"

"How does a maid look like?" asked Maria.

The old concubine burst into a laugh that resonated with the palace walls covered with unique tiles.

"It seems that we'll have a good time with you. I haven't laughed like that in a long time. Welcome, Maria. Bring those big bags from the corner and listen to me carefully. You will find out where they have brought you."

46

"The Harem is the home of the Sultan. I think you know who the Sultan is." Maria responded with a laugh and thought that the old concubine was once a very beautiful woman, although there was a deep scar on her face, which was extending from her left ear to her chin. After a long time, she felt safe for the first time.

"I know," said Maria.

"Well, at least we won't start from the beginning. Rich people like your Pasha can have their own harem. So anyone who has money, who can buy slaves, can have a Harem. The Harem is the place where the Sultan lives his private life. The Harem has always been an interesting subject for those outside the Palace. The Harem is always thought of as a place which is full of women and where the Sultans have sex. Since no foreigners were permitted to enter it by themselves, imaginations ran about what sort of debauchery happened behind the doors of Harem. They wrote fanciful books and drew pictures. Anyone, who reads those books and sees those pictures, imagines an illusive Harem. However, none of them are true. Moreover, the harem is not an institution unique to the Ottoman Empire. There were also harems in the pre-Ottoman states."

The old concubine hesitated. "Do you understand what I'm saying?" she asked.

"I understand," Maria said vaguely. Did this concubine have a story like her? She didn't want to piss her off, but she couldn't stop asking. "How do you know all of this?"

"From the books," the old concubine said calmly. Maria was relieved that she was not angry.

"Soon your lessons will begin. The Harem is also a school. You can find the rarest books here. You can't find them anywhere else in the world. Since they sent you to the laundry, you'll have plenty of time for reading at night. You can read with me a lot."

Although this answer didn't satisfy Maria, she didn't express it.

"So how long does the Ottoman Empire have a Harem?" she asked. While opening the new laundry bags and throwing the contents into the hot water.

The old concubine continued to tell.

"It is said that The Ottoman Harem was founded during the reign of Sultan Orhan Gazi, who was the second Sultan of the Empire. But his father, Osman Gazi who was the founder of the empire, had also a harem. But the women of the harem were not slaves at that time. They were his wives."

"Wouldn't a woman object to her husband marrying other women?"

"It is said that in the time of Osman Gazi, although the state was small, the house of the Sultan had many chores which one woman couldn't cope with. So the Sultan needed more than one woman. Also, those women would be ashamed of objecting to their husband according to traditions."

Maria couldn't believe the things which the old concubine told. How could a woman accept to share her husband with another woman? But she didn't want to discuss the old traditions.

The tired concubine sat down in her chair and asked Maria to bring her some water, pointing to the jug behind her.

"You made me talk a lot, my throat dried up," she said.

The old concubine continued to tell after drinking water.

"After 1413, during the reign of Sultan Çelebi Mehmet, the Harem was truly institutionalized and gained its present quality. When you say harem, don't just think of women. There are also officials of the Harem. The most important of these officials are called the 'Haremağası'. They are also called as 'Darüssaade Ağaları'. You must have seen them when you arrived. These men are mostly black eunuchs. I will tell about them later. This is, in fact, parallel to the settlement of the state. Since the state has also been institutionalized since then, the Harem has also become institutionalized. Of course, as the state grows, the harem grows in parallel. The peak point of the

Harem was at the period of Sultan Murat the third. That is after the year 1574."

Maria was very confused. If the Harem was the home of the Sultan, why had it to be institutionalized?

"What does the peak point of the Harem mean?" asked Maria.

The old concubine raised her eyebrows and said ironically, "You've just been lazy from the first day. You're avoiding work by making me talk. Come on. Look outside the door. Are there any new bags? Can the 600-year-old laundry of the Ottoman Empire be finished?"

47

Even though they seemed to be engrossed in different parts of the room, the other girls, all of whom listened curiously, understood very well what the old concubine meant.

After the new laundry bags were opened and thrown into boiling water, the old concubine continued, "The peak point of the Harem means an increase in the number of women and eunuchs. There are concubines serving to the Sultan's mother, sisters, and favorite concubines as well as the Sultan himself. The Ottomans have an interesting feature. They record and store everything about the Palace. You can see the amount and prices of potatoes and onions which were bought for the palace a hundred years ago. Even they keep the love letters of the Sultans, and also the records of what they had eaten and had drunk in the palace. For example, there are books containing the harem population in the palace. There are books showing the expenditures made for the harem. Don't be fooled by today's conditions of the harem. Once there were two or three hundred women in the palace. But as I said, they're not just taken to serve to the Sultan. They are also used in other services. There have been concubines, who have lived in the palace for the rest of their lives and have never seen a Sultan, a Prince, a Valide Sultan or other Sultans."

"Have you ever seen a Sultan?" asked Maria, but when her sentence was over, she had regretted it.

The old concubine said, "The Harem is no longer as crowded as before. The first period of the Harem is not mentioned much, even the public does not know. Because at that time, Harem was not active in state life. So it did not interfere with government affairs."

"Are they getting involved now?" asked Maria.

The old concubine smiled again. She thought that this newcomer girl didn't know anything. It was obvious that they sent her to the laundry from the first day.

"Is there any State left to interfere?" she replied in short.

Meanwhile, the sound of the Afternoon Prayer began to echo on the walls of the Harem.

"Soon the girls will start to come here," said the old concubine. "Who will come?" Maria asked with a bit of curiosity and a little fear. "I am sure you know what the 'call to prayer' is. You must have learned it in Pasha's house. But of course, if your Pasha is a Muslim."

In fact, this question of the concubine was very cynical. Although many Pashas appeared to be Muslims, none of them abandoned their old religions.

48

Footsteps were heard in the hallway. Five concubines came in. They all greeted the old concubine with extreme respect and sat on the wooden bench by the wall. Maria was trying to hide her admiration as she watched them with surprised eyes. They were all very beautiful girls, in extremely beautiful clothes. She did not understand what they were talking about. Because they were speaking in Turkish. First, they took off their shoes and started to rub their tired feet. It was obvious that they told each other how tired they were.

The tall, slender, beautiful girl looked at Maria thoroughly. When Maria began to fear that the young girl might have recognized her, she wondered what she had to do.

"What's your name? Are you a newcomer?" asked the young concubine.

The old concubine intervened and said, "Yes she has just arrived this morning. She doesn't speak Turkish. She understands only Russian."

Maria could only say, "Yes, I came this morning."

As the old concubine guessed what the girls could say and think, she began to speak without allowing them to talk.

"Don't worry, girls. Since they sent her to the laundry room on her first day, she can't be your rival."

One of them said, "Such an old girl can only rival you."

The old concubine was accustomed to these quarrels but she thought that Maria was not used to those and that her heart might break. However, in the last period of her life, Maria had been dealing with these kinds of behaviors from much more dangerous and armed people. So Maria didn't care about her. She kept spinning the clothes in the boiling water.

The old concubine who took the laundry gavel from the floor said, "Now I will crush your heads with this and stick them to the wall. How many times have I told you not to mess with my girls? Get out of here. Don't try to disturb my girls anymore."

"Oh, Gülnihal, shouldn't we have some fun? We're tired of running around the palace all day. Don't get mad. Ok, we won't disturb her anymore," said one of the concubines and tried to soften the conversation.

"I haven't heard anyone get into the Harem lately. Where did you come from?" asked another concubine.

"Pasha sent me here."

"Which Pasha?" the concubine continued to ask.

The old concubine intervened because she knew that these questions would not end if she did not intervene now. "Look at her. She asks as if she knows all the Pashas. Mind your own business. Where are my coffee and dessert? If you haven't brought anything, get out now."

"Okay do not be mad. Nihan cooks on the stove and soon brings. I see that you are eager to send us when you find a new friend," said the concubine who just asked Maria her name. The old concubine understood the taunts underlying these words, but she didn't want to give the answer she deserved near Maria.

And the old concubine gave a very sarcastic response.

"Winter seems to never end on your nights. I guess spring doesn't stop by."

With these words, the old concubine revealed that she knew the sexual relations of that concubine with the other girls. She was surprised that how the old concubine, who had not been out of the laundry all day, knew about them. She was afraid that her relationship might have been learned by everyone in the Harem.

"If you don't want others to throw stones at you, you mustn't throw stones at anyone. Come on, get my coffee, or get lost," said the old concubine lastly with the enjoyment of the victory that she won.

49

After drinking coffee and eating desserts, the guest concubines left the laundry room one by one. Maria looked at the old concubine and asked if her name was Gülnihal. "Yes," said the old concubine.

"But don't ask who I was before I became Gulnihal. Because I don't know and I don't remember."

She remembered. When she was only thirteen, she remembered how her parents sold her to the slave traders, saying that "You'll be a princess. You'll be a queen. You'll save all of us from this miserable life."

She just didn't want to remember.

"Aren't these girls Muslim? How can they come here at prayer time?" asked Maria.

"You can't use Muslim girls as concubines. Islam is taught here but no one is converted to Islam. Being a Muslim means being a free person. So during prayer times, some of them leave their apprentices at work and go to some quiet corners to find some rest. Just like I left you the laundry job now." She laughed and pointed at Maria's gavel at the same time.

Maria laughed too. She didn't complain about doing laundry work. She would get bored if she sat down without doing anything. "You were telling about the harem. If you are not bored, will you continue?" asked Maria.

Gülnihal smiled. "The Harem began to come into prominence and became spoken with Hurrem Sultan, who was the wife of Suleyman the Magnificent. Harem's involvement in state affairs began with Hurrem Sultan. Then she was followed by Mihrimah Sultan who was her daughter, Nurbanu Sultan during the reign of Sultan Murad the third and Safiye Sultan. They all took active roles in state affairs. In the 17th century, during the reign of Kösem Sultan, the Harem was more effective than ever in the state administration. It is thought that the reign of women brought the end of the empire. Even Hammer used very harsh statements about women being effective in management."

While Maria was going to ask the old lady how she knew Hammer, she stopped because the old lady could ask her how she knew him.

Suddenly Gülnihal changed the subject and said, "Normally, they do not classify newly arrived concubines without giving basic education. They probably thought that you couldn't be a favorite concubine. And they sent you directly to the laundry department."

She started to smile again and continued, "Don't get mad, but they send the problematic ones to the laundry. Just like me."

"What do you mean?"

"Do you see the scar on my face? It happened here."

"How did it happen?"

"There are two types of weapons in the harem. Dagger and poison. Don't ask any more questions. A concubine wanted to kill me. At night in the dormitory, she attacked me with a dagger and lacerated my face. I jumped on her and took the dagger from her and stabbed her. I didn't mean to kill her. But at that moment, I was blind from anger. I didn't know what I was doing. I thought they'd kill me. Then someone told Valide Sultan the truth. They sent me to the laundry. I've been here ever since. Don't ask any more questions about it. Why did your Pasha give up on you? Did Pasha buy new concubines?"

"No. I was not in the Pasha's harem in the sense you mean. My job was just cleaning the house. One day, a British officer came to Pasha's house. He asked Pasha to hand over the house to him. Of course, Pasha did not accept this and threw out the men from the house. That evening there was an attack on the house. The attackers set the house on fire. One of them entered the room where we slept. The man attacked the girl I was staying with. Meanwhile, I was washing my hands in the bathroom. When I went out and saw the man trying to rape her, I grabbed the dagger from the drawer and stabbed him. The girl and I jumped out of the window into the garden. There was smoke everywhere. We could hardly breathe. Several neighbors gathered and tried to extinguish the fire. We knew secret exit doors in the garden, so we managed to get out of the house. We hugged each other and started to watch. I thought of running away at that moment, but I had nowhere to go.

Both Pasha and his family were very good people, I was wondering what would happen to them. Fortunately, the officers took control of the incident. When Pasha and his family went out of the house, we went near them. We went to the house of one of the relatives of Pasha with the officers. We spent the night there, but no one slept. Pasha and his relatives talked fervently until the morning. In the morning, Pasha told us that, it was no longer possible for him to stay in Istanbul. He would go to Anatolia and he would entrust us to the people he knew. And I was sent here."

"So you're a murderer too."

Maria paused for a moment and said, "I don't know if he's dead, but I hope he's dead."

Maria had taken revenge for all the tortures, insults and humiliations, especially those that had been done on that last night, for months and months from that murderous villain.

She had stabbed repeatedly. She had regained consciousness after the screams of the other girl in the room. Then, in an unbelievable composure, she took the girl with her and stepped out of the window. Maria intended to run away with the other girl. But she did not want to leave her brother's grave, which she had buried in the garden of the Pasha's house. What would happen to the grave if she left?

The old concubine saw the change in Maria's face. It was as if someone else had come to replace that naive and innocent girl. Gülnihal had noticed the frighteningness of Maria's silence from the very first moment she had come to the laundry room.

"Since we're here together, go and cook a Turkish coffee," said Gülnihal. Maria said okay but she didn't know where to find the coffee, where to cook it and how to cook it. One of the other concubines who understood Maria's helplessness said, "Come with me. I will teach you."

They entered through the narrow door.

"I didn't even realize that there was a door here," said Maria.

The concubine turned to her with a smile and said, "This is the Ottoman Palace. Here, you never know which door will open and where it will lead."

50

With the comfort of having completed their jobs, Gülnihal continued to tell while three women were sitting together and drinking their coffee.

"There are houses where female slaves are sold. Rich women buy slaves from those houses. Since the sellers are male, when the female customer enters, the seller goes out and waits. If she wants to buy a slave, she'll tell her coachman. The coachman negotiates with the seller and makes the delivery. There are slaves sent as gifts to the Harem just like you. The

Pashas send gifts to the palace to rise in the state levels. It seems that your Pasha didn't give you any good references, so they sent you directly to the laundry."

Upon Gulnihal's allusive remarks, they all started to laugh. Maria was getting used to Gülnihal's jokes. For the first time after that night, she was able to chat with someone and had fun. Nevertheless, her family and the things happened to them did not leave her mind for a moment. Maria was feeling guilty when she laughed.

"Was the Harem always in this palace?" asked Maria.

"The sultans lived in 3 palaces in Istanbul. The first is Topkapı, the second is Dolmabahce, and the third is the Yıldız Palace. Now we are in Yıldız Palace."

Thus Maria had learned the name of the Palace where she was brought. Although the palace had become synonymous with sadness and tears for her, she smiled a little as her memories of her childhood came to life. Suddenly, the huge dancing balls came to her mind and she remembered how hundreds of people danced in perfect harmony with the finest pieces of classical music played by a wonderful orchestra.

Suddenly Maria asked, "Do they drink alcohol in the Harem?"

Although she had regretted after asking this question, her new friends did not miss this opportunity and they had already started to make fun of Maria.

"How did this come to your mind?" asked Gülnihal.

And the other girl asked with exaggerated respect, "What would you like to drink, my Sultan?" and they started laughing again.

"It just came to my mind" said Maria and she laughed at herself.

The old concubine continued to speak, "They say that Sultan Abdulhamid the second used to drink rum. He even told that rum was not contrary to Islamic rules. And only wine was mentioned in the Qur'an. When a man wants to do something, he always finds a solution. People forget that the Sultans are also human beings. They think that Sultans are divine creatures. In addition to the life they live as a Sultan, these people also have private lives."

Maria was surprised that a concubine, who was doing laundry all day in a room which looked like a small warehouse, had such a wide range of judgment. She began to wonder more about Gülnihal, but she hesitated to ask.

Gülnihal continued to tell, "From Sultan Selim the first, the Ottoman Sultans were also caliphs. And some of the Sultans were drinking alcohol. The most well-known of these are Sultan Yıldırım Beyazıt and Sultan Murat the fourth. But the alcohol which was bought for the palace was not recorded in the kitchen book. During the reign of Sultan Abdulhamid the second, the records of the alcoholic drinks in the culinary books of the Palace were recorded only during the visit of Kaiser Wilhelm the second. Other than that, it was never recorded. However, when the Sultan wants to drink rum, he doesn't tell his officers to buy rum."

Maria could not help herself and ask with a laugh. "Where does the alcohol come from? Does the Sultan go out and buy it?"

Gülnihal and the other concubine were now accustomed to Maria's questions. They smiled too.

The other concubine said, "I'll take these laundries to dry. Senior concubine will start to grunt now."

Gülnihal continued, "They bring it from abroad. The ambassadors or the Pashas who are sent abroad by the Sultan, bring special alcoholic drinks to the Sultan. Both the father and the mother of Sultan Abdulhamid the second died from tuberculosis at an early age. Rumors of the Sultan drinking rum spread in the Harem. His doctor warned Sultan Abdulhamid the second and said that his mother and father both died of tuberculosis and he wouldn't have a long life. Although Sultan Abdulhamid said that he stopped drinking after the doctor's warning, he continued to drink."

Maria took some courage from the long conversation and finally asked the question that had stuck in her mind for hours. "Don't get me wrong, but you've been sitting here all day and washing clothes. When and how do you learn all of these?"

"Have you been thinking about this since?", she said with a loud laugh.

"I've been talking in vain for hours. Keep in mind. This is the center of a 600-year-old empire. The harem is its heart. All kinds of news come from all over the world. Besides, concubines and eunuchs are very good at listening behind the closed doors. Fabric saleswomen and jewelers who come to the palace tell all the rumors which are spoken in the city. Keep in mind while you're here. It is never known with whom the concubines meet and who they know."

"Do you have any spies at the palace for information?" asked Maria curiously. Gülnihal responded only with a cynical smile.

Then she suddenly appeared angry to change the subject, "Where's that lazy bitch? It is almost evening prayer time. Our food hasn't arrived yet. She must be flirting with the Bostancıbaşı again."

Maria was surprised and asked, "Who is Bostancıbaşı?"

"They are Palace Guards."

"Are they being castrated too?"

"Oh, Maria. Finally, they took pity on me and sent you here to cheer me up. No, they're soldiers. They are not eunuchs."

"Then how can the concubines meet with them?"

"I told you. You can never know with whom the concubines meet. Anyway, I get angry when my food is late. I will tell you later."

It was obvious that the old concubine was getting angry.

"I can stay here alone if you want to go to dinner. Do not worry. I don't mess around," said Maria.

"We're not allowed to go out of the laundry room. The newest concubine brings the dinner here. From now on you will bring dinner to us. So you must learn how to do it. You can get out of here in three ways, either when you get married, when you get infectious diseases or when you die. We leave the laundry room only in bedtime. Laundry is the exile of the harem. You better get used to it."

51

Maria did not understand why she was given directly to the laundry room. Was she too old for the Harem, as they say? If I was old for the harem, why did Pasha send me to the harem? She had lived in captivity for months. And now, as Gülnihal said, she could only get out of here when she died or when she had an infectious disease. However, the man who brought her to Istanbul said that when the war was over he would pick her up. If Pasha left Istanbul, as he said, how would he find her? You're naive, Maria. How could you trust a stranger you've seen for the first time in your life?

Then suddenly, her brother's grave came to her mind. They buried him in the backyard of Pasha's Mansion with a simple ceremony. After the war, she would take him home and give him the ceremony he deserved. Did the men who occupied Pasha's house give comfort to his grave? Suddenly she felt a chill on her back. Ornate walls covered with blue tiles began to suffocate her. At that moment she realized that it was too ornamented for a simple launderette. The pearl inlaid furniture, gold leaf stools, and the tools they used were very ornamented. She was used to it, but she was surprised that the room was so fancy. She wondered the Sultan's rooms.

52

A young concubine came in with a large tray in her hand. Gülnihal, who was very angry when she got hungry, started to scold her.

"Where have you been? Do we have to wait for your flirting? I am starving."

"No, I swear to God. The eunuch took me to work. We cleaned the room of the Little Sultan. Whatever I said, he didn't leave me."

"Do not tell me fairy tales. Doesn't the Sultan have her own concubines?" Then she turned to Maria and said, "I hope you will not be like them. Otherwise, we will not get along."

The concubine turned to Maria and said, "You must be the new concubine. My name is Feranaz."

Maria didn't understand anything because she said it in Turkish. Gülnihal intervened, "She only speaks in Russian."

However, Maria knew many other languages besides Russian, which unfortunately did not include Turkish. She had learned a little Turkish during her stay in Pasha's house. Feranaz, like many concubines in the harem, loved to have fun with girls who did not speak Turkish. She thought that new entertainment came out and then repeated the same words in Russian.

Feranaz brought the small table, put the tray on it and opened the lids of the pots. Maria had forgotten that she hadn't eaten for hours in excitement and curiosity. She remembered her hunger with the exquisite smell of the soup. There was a wonderful tomato soup with rice and a meat dish that she hadn't eaten before.

After dinner, Feranaz told Maria, "Let's take the tray together. And I'll show you around."

Gülnihal understood that Maria had been asked not to be around much as she was sent directly to the laundry room.

"No. You can show her later. She must stay here until bedtime."

Thinking that the chances of establishing authority on a new concubine decreased, Feranaz got angry but could not say anything. Feranaz and Gül went out to leave the pots in the kitchen. Gül aimed to learn the latest gossips about the new girl.

"You didn't ask the name of the meal. Have you eaten it before?" asked Gülnihal.

"I was so hungry I didn't even think of it. I haven't eaten all day," replied Maria.

Gülnihal was not sure that Maria was only a cleaner. She had suspicions about her. It was obvious that she was not like any other concubines because of her speech style and behaviors. Was that why she was deported to the laundry room on her first day?

Feranaz and Gül came back. Gül was the laundry guard that night. Maria was very surprised by the night shift in the laundry room. Then when they told her that there was a night shift in every section of the palace, she thought it was a good opportunity to meet with 'Bostancıbaşı' and she smiled.

Maria was surprised even more on her way to the bedroom. The palace was magnificent with amazing ornaments. "Everything you see in yellow is gold," said Gülnihal. Maria was accustomed to them, but she was fascinated by the beauty of the Arabic scripts on the walls. This palace had something else. It was a small palace, but full of works of art that she had never seen before. The palace was seemed depressive to her. But maybe it was just a reflection of her own sorrow.

When they arrived in the dormitory, Gülnihal introduced her to Kalfa. Kalfa knew about Maria. She showed her the room where she could take her new clothes and then she took her to the room on the right end of the corridor. After Maria left, Gülnihal began to question Kalfa.

"Who brought this girl? Why did you send her directly to the laundry room?"

"Calm down, Gulnihal. Did she piss you off? There is nothing to worry about. The Head of the eunuchs was very busy today. He was with Valide Sultan all day. I didn't want to disturb him for a single concubine. So I sent her to you. So she wouldn't walk around."

Then she walked away after saying goodnight to Gülnihal.

Gülnihal's suspicions increased with the sudden departure of the Kalfa without allowing her to ask another question. She knew the unwritten rules of the Harem very well and didn't insist on it. But she was convinced that she was right in her suspicions.

53

Maria took her clothes from the first room on the left and then went to the room which was shown to her. There were three other girls in the room. It was obvious that they were also new in the harem. But the good part was that all three of them spoke in Russian. Maria greeted them and introduced herself. She wanted to go to bed and sleep as soon as possible.

Her past experiences did not put her to sleep for a long time. She was constantly thinking of taking revenge or committing suicide.

She remembered that she did not go to the bathroom. She asked the girls if they knew where the toilet was. One of the girls described it briefly. As far as Maria understood, there was a marble stepped room at the beginning of the corridor. She took the little oil lamp and left the room. As soon as she left the room, she saw a black man with his hands on his waist. She took a step back from fear and fell.

The man started to laugh at first. But when he saw the oil lamp on the floor, he got angry and started shouting.

"Clumsy woman. Look what you did. Why haven't you slept already?"

And he hit the ground with the stick in his hand. As the other concubines tried to understand what was happening, the Harem was in complete silence. Maria didn't understand anything that the man said to her. The man was angry. But she didn't understand what he was upset about. Was it forbidden to leave the room or go to the bathroom?

Gulnihal was watching everything from the other side of the corridor. She came near the eunuch. She told him that the girl was new and couldn't understand Turkish. Then she turned to Maria and asked what the problem was. While Gülnihal started talking, the eunuch turned to Maria and started talking in Russian.

"You don't know how to walk yet. How do you expect to get into the Sultan's bed? Get out!"

Maria was standing still with the oil lamp in her hand. She didn't know whether she had to go to the bathroom or go back to her room. Gülnihal pointed to the side of the toilet with her eyes. Maria finally found what she was looking for when she saw the marble steps and pushed the two-winged wooden door. Illuminated with a few dim candles, the room was covered with white marble from the ceiling to the floor.

"God! Where am I? What am I doing here?" Maria asked herself, and she prayed to God for the man to come and save her.

As she left the toilet, she went quickly to her room to avoid encountering the eunuch again. She thought the girls were asleep or they were pretending to sleep. Without looking around, she went straight into her bed, to the right of the entrance, and closed her eyes.

54

Maria felt shaking on her shoulders. When she barely opened her eyes, she saw Feranaz. "Am I asleep?" she asked. Feranaz gestured to be quiet with her hand.

"We gathered with the girls downstairs, chatting. They wonder about you. Come, I'll take you to them. Just be quiet, let's not wake the others," said Feranaz silently. Maria was sleepy when she stood up. As she attempted to change her outfit, Feranaz grabbed her arm firmly and said, "No need to change your clothes."

While walking after Feranaz, Maria asked, "Why don't you call the other girls? Aren't they curious about them?"

"Gülnihal just asked me to call you," replied Feranaz.

Maria whispered as they came down one floor, "I am afraid of getting caught by the eunuch again. I will meet everybody tomorrow."

"Don't worry. Nobody is around here at this hour. We gather every night," said Feranaz.

Although she tried to get to know her surroundings and where she was, Maria couldn't see anything because of the darkness. They stopped in front of a wooden door.

"Get inside and meet the girls. I will go to the kitchen and bring some food." Maria doubted for a moment whether to go in or not. But then she entered in while taking a deep breath. As soon as the door slammed shut, the guns started to explode.

When Maria opened her eyes from a nightmare in fear, she found herself on the floor. First, she glanced around to see where she was. The door was knocked very hard. The person behind the door shouted in a harsh voice. One of the other girls got up and opened the door. The woman at the door continued to shout in Russian.

"Rise! You can't stay here too much with this laziness."

Then she saw Maria lying on the floor.

"Oh! my Sultan. I think you decided to continue your beauty sleep on the ground."

Then she turned back, "Get up quickly, get ready to go to the bath. Take all of your clothes with you," she shouted and left the room.

55

Maria and the other girls hurriedly dressed up, and when they came out of the room as quickly as they could, they saw Kalfa and followed her. After leaving the corridor where the rooms were located, she called one of the concubines and said, "Take these girls to the kitchen and then to the hammam."

After greeting Kalfa with respect, the young concubine pointed at the girls to follow her. Maria tried to find out how many floors the palace had, and the location of the room they were sleeping in, but she could not be orientated, which increased her shyness and insecurity. On their way to the kitchen, she saw a door which was similar to the one she saw in her nightmare. She suddenly shuddered and thought about Feranaz.

They finally came to the kitchen after passing through the corridors of the palace which were identical to each other. It was a small kitchen for employees only. The young concubine pointed to the small table on the floor. There was a woman in the kitchen who was cutting cheese. She ordered her to prepare breakfast for the newcomer girls. And she asked a cup of coffee for herself.

She sat in the luminous corner on the left side of the kitchen. Maria's attention was drawn to the concubine's obedience to the Kalfa and the authoritarian stance to the cook. But in both cases concubine's confident attitude was remarkable. She seemed like someone who didn't talk too much. She was able to express her wishes with gestures. She suddenly realized that all women were wearing different clothes. She thought this place was just like an army. Everyone was classified according to their rank and seniority. A little later she heard the cook's harsh voice.

"Are our Sultans waiting for their food at their feet? Get up and get them!" All four girls stood up and took their plates, forks and knives, jugs and glasses full of milk and settled down on the floor.

Maria ate on the floor for the second time in her life. She thought it was like having a picnic. While eating the breakfast-like dough and bread-like dishes that she had never seen or tasted before, Maria once again saw that every item in the palace was thought to the finest detail.

She had seen such items before, but in a simple little kitchen, everything from the carpet on the floor to the 'sini' which they put their food on it, from the jug to the glasses, the plates were in harmony. She thought of it as a magnificent painting from the hands of a master artist.

Then she turned his head to the left and looked at the concubine that brought them to the kitchen more carefully. She thought that the young concubine was the most important figure in completing the painting. The young concubine looked as if she was practicing a religious ritual with her restrained and balanced movements while sipping her coffee.

Then Maria began to examine the clothes of the young concubine. It was obvious that the cloth of the young concubine was very high quality. The embroidery that resembled rivers flowing from the high mountains converged on the woman's uterus and formed a center. It was almost as if the springs of life that went to the source of life and spread from there to the universe were depicted.

She began to wonder whether that was a simple model test or a thoughtful model. Time seemed to have stopped for Maria while staring at her. The young concubine looked like a newly blooming seed with the lights of the morning sun beginning to glide through the latticed glass behind her. She looked more like a Princess than a slave with her outfit and manners.

56

When she saw the sunlight, she realized that they had been awakened before the sun came up. Then her nightmare came to her mind. She thought of Feranaz. Should she be paying attention to Feranaz? After a while, they heard the voice of the young concubine.

"Come on. Hurry up. We are getting late."

While the four girls rose from the floor and went to the concubine, the voice of the cook was heard this time.

"Where do you think you're going without collecting your dishes? I'm not your maid," she shouted.

The young concubine showed the large tray on the counter with her hand and said, "Put them all on that and take it behind the counter."

Three of the girls were looking at the young concubine with fearful eyes because they didn't speak any Turkish. Maria took the tray and walked through the door to the left of the counter. Inside, she saw other girls. Some of them were washing the dishes and some of them were cleaning the floor. She asked one of the dishwashers what to do with the tray. She pointed to the stall closest to the entrance and told Maria to leave it there. Maria didn't know whether to wash the dishes, so she started to wait. The dishwasher girl told Maria to leave. Otherwise, she would be late. Maria went out without saying a word.

When they started chasing the young concubine, Maria realized that they had never talked to each other with her roommates after the first night. Maybe it's best not to talk, she thought to herself. The silence of the palace caught Maria's attention as they were following the concubine.

There was no sound from any room they passed. If there weren't a few concubines they met on the way, there seemed to be no sign of life. When they reached the end of a long corridor, the young concubine stopped. She gestured for them to wait. That should be the source of silence, she thought for a moment, as the young concubine constantly addressed them with hand and head signs.

Since everyone came from different places, she thought that they wouldn't understand each other and should be talking in sign language. The concubine strictly instructed them not to raise their heads and eyes from the ground after entering the door, to give greetings by gently bending their knees when they stopped after the entrance, and to unite their hands in front of them and never open them unintentionally. No matter what, they would never talk unless asked.

57

The concubine knocked on the door three times. As soon as the door was opened, an exquisite smell spread outwards. Maria didn't know what it was, and it was unlike any of the fragrances she had known before.

The fragrances were dominant throughout the palace, but this time it was so intense and beautiful. She would learn the mysterious language and signs of the palace in the future. But all of this would remain mysterious to her for a while. Although this obscurity sometimes disturbed her, she didn't care much because she had no connection with life as in the old times.

The young concubine entered first. At the end of the spacious room, the young concubine stood three steps away from the woman who was sitting on the sofa and writing something on a paper in front of her.

She said something after joining her hands over her belly, gently breaking her knees and bowing her head forward. The young concubine walked back and came up to the door, as the sitting woman shook her head slightly to confirm by her head. She gestured for Maria and her friends to come in.

Maria, who was very curious about the content of the room, had already started examining inside as much as she could see through the doorway. There was nothing in the middle of the room, except dome-like brassware at a height that could reach her waist.

There were sofas along the walls. The old woman was in front of the window which was covered with cages like spider webs. Then as far as she could see, there was calligraphy on the walls written in the Arabic alphabet. They were very fancy. She was very curious about what was written in them.

The girls came in silently in order as they did not know where to stand. The young concubine stopped them with a stiff hand sign after they passed a bit of the fireplace-like item standing in the middle of the room. They were told to line up. The old concubine examined the girls one by one, just lifting her eyes a little bit from the papers in front of her. Then she began to speak with a lip gesture impressing that she didn't like what she saw.

"Are these the concubines who are accepted as the future mothers of holy Princes? They don't deserve walking even ten steps behind Hurrem Sultan. It is necessary to cut the heads of those who accepted these girls to the Palace to make an example."

Other than Maria, the other three girls could not understand anything because she was talking in Turkish.

Maria was listening, but she didn't hear what the old concubine said. Her eyes were on the carpet. She has never seen one like that before. Walking on it made her feel like she was flying.

Who was that old woman? A slave could not have such a magnificent room. As the old concubine began to speak Russian, Maria listened to her attentively this time.

"Take these dirty girls to the hammam. Let them wash thoroughly. Then have the physician examine them. Be sure that they will not bring the dirt from their villages to the holy gate of our Sultan."

58

When the young concubine quickly began to walk back, the girls followed her. The tallest of the girls hit the sofa next to her and fell. She didn't know what to do out of fear. She was getting more confused as she tried to stand up in a hurry. After that, she stepped onto her dress and fell again. Though they thought the old concubine would be very angry, she just smiled bitterly. Then she asked one of the concubines standing by the wall to tidy up the mess.

When they left the room, the face of the girl who had fallen to the ground had become pale white. She was trembling out of fear and barely breathing.

Although the young concubine looked at her as if she were going to kill her at first, she didn't say anything later on. They quickly walked away from there and stopped at the door of the Hamman which was downstairs.

The young concubine knocked the door again three times and the door opened again from the inside. As soon as it opened, exquisite odors were spread out, along with slight steam. Maria thought that every part of the palace must have its distinctive fragrance.

After talking to the woman inside the hammam, the young concubine went out without saying anything. The woman she spoke with told them to undress after examining the girls from head to toe.

The floor and the walls were completely made of marble. The hammam was very hot and steamy. Maria realized for a moment that she was barely breathing.

Although the woman in the hammam talked in Russian, the girls were moving so slowly. Because they did not have any idea where to put their dresses and where to proceed. They were also afraid to ask questions.

Thereupon, the woman shouted with a harsh tone.

"Take them off, I can't wait for you all day!"

They began to take off their clothes quickly. This time they did not raise their heads from the ground because they were ashamed of their nudities. They didn't look at each other, nor the woman.

"You," she said, touching the shoulder of the tallest girl. "Open the top lid of the closet behind you. Bring the sack inside."

When the girl turned around to do what she said, she saw that there were five doors at the top of the closet and stared at the woman with begging eyes.

The concubine grimaced as if she were staring at a disgusting creature and said, "Open one of them. It doesn't matter."

The girl quickly did what she said, and brought a very elegant sack covered in leather.

The concubine turned to the girls and said, "Throw all of your old clothes into this."

Maria couldn't help herself when they started throwing their clothes in the sack. "I have no other clothes. Don't they mix up in there? Can't I keep my necklace and bracelets? They are souvenirs from my mother," she asked desperately.

Maria's question made the concubine even angrier. "Do you think you can live here with the dirt and germs you bring from the outside? They will all be burned."

Maria thought that her necklace and bracelets would be burned for a moment.

The concubine continued, "Take off your necklace and bracelets. Take them with you. You can put them on again after being washed and examined."

59

Meanwhile, the woman began to carefully examine Maria's body. Especially the scars on Maria's belly and legs had attracted the attention of the concubine. After looking more carefully, she saw a lot of scratches all over her body. She asked for her name and, after nodding her head, indicating that she would never forget the answer, told them to get inside.

Although it was very hot inside, all four girls were trembling out of fear again. There was no one around. They didn't know who or what they were waiting for. All four were ashamed of their naked state. They lined up side by side to avoid seeing each other, and with an instinct, they crossed their hands over their groins. They looked like prisoners who had been sentenced to death waiting for their executioners. Meanwhile, without raising her head, Maria looked at the other three girls with the tip of an eye and realized for the first time how young they were.

As Gülnihal said, she was the oldest among them. What happened to her in the last year was not something that anyone could easily handle. The things that she experienced had battered and aged her body and appearance as well as her soul. She thought the oldest of the other girls should be fifteen years old at most. Then she remembered herself at that age. The games she played with her siblings, the trips they took as a family.

These girls were just little kids. The girl standing right next to her should have been thirteen years old at most. She felt sorry for the girls at first but then she realized that she was in the same situation.

60

The first thing that ended the silence in the bath was footsteps. As the footsteps heard much more loudly than they should be due to the echo, the girls' heartbeat accelerated.

From the left-hand corner, a fat white woman, with her hair gathered and her body covered with loincloth from chest to knees, approached with a smile.

She began to speak sarcastically.

"So you are the new candidates. Take loincloth, soap, and clogs from the room behind the fountain and start to wash yourselves. Be quick!"

The girls, who did not speak any Turkish, looked at Maria again, bewildered. Maria gestured for them to follow her. Hundreds of loincloths were arranged very carefully on the shelves behind the fountain, and soaps were placed on the shelves on the wall to the right.

There were embroidered clogs, each of which seemed to be a work of art. With Maria's sign, all the girls took one of each and started to wait. Maria was standing in front of the soaps, absorbing those wonderful scents, trying to figure out what they were made of.

She remembered her childhood. The forest walks with her family, wandering among the orchards, and tasting each one by one. While every familiar scent reminded her of other good memories, she heard a scream from inside the hammam.

They were told to hurry. The scream turned those fragrances into gunpowder. They all ran and lined up in front of her.

"Don't waste my time. Come on, wash up and get rid of your dirt."

61

The four girls sat in the palace bath, facing the wall and facing the fountains. There was a one-meter distance between each girl. They started pouring hot water on their heads. Maria, who had just woken up from her dreams, with the scream of a concubine, began to examine her surroundings more carefully.

She noticed that the bath was like an old pantheon. The circle-shaped structure and the perforated dome on the ceiling were very similar to the pantheon she had seen before.

Were they the virgin victims prepared to be dedicated to God? Since the kings are God's representatives on earth, she thought that they were going to be gifted to God.

Then she stared at the girls, who were lined up to the right and the left. They were washing themselves as quickly as they could without raising their heads.

They were all very beautiful girls. Each one's body looked perfect. The girl to her left was only thirteen years old. She didn't have nipples yet. Maria relieved. While there were these young girls, they would not offer an old concubine like her to God. She smiled.

For a moment, she imagined that little girl in Sultan's bed. She was presenting herself to the Sultan. He must be old and ugly. She thought even that idea was disgusting.

How could a girl make love with someone she doesn't feel anything about? How can she touch him, how can she kiss him? Or how does she feel as that man touches her?

Then she suddenly thought of the handsome man she met in Romania. She didn't know anything but his name. She had forgotten these beautiful feelings due to her severe traumas. Or because she felt that there would be disrespect to her family's memory, she had suppressed her feelings with the psychology of guilt.

"What if I left the ballroom with him? What kind of life would I have?" she asked herself.

The first time she entered the ballroom, she noticed a tall young man in his white jacket and the same color shirt, shining like a diamond. He was chatting with a young man of the same age next to him in the distant corner of the hall with his shot glass.

She remembered the moment they met. It felt as if time had stopped and there were only two on Earth. With her mother's call, the hall suddenly became crowded and the loud voices covered the room all over again. The young man was no longer there when she looked back at the same place after talking to her mother.

With the start of the dances, they walked towards the doors opening to the large balcony of the hall with her sister to get some air and talk. She was looking at almost everyone's face. But she couldn't see the young man's face again. Or was it an instant dream? She thought she was hallucinating from fatigue.

62

Maria and her sister got to the balcony. It was a beautiful night. The stars were brighter, more crowded and closer to each other. She stared at the stars for a long time. She was waiting impatiently and with excitement for a falling star so that she could hold a wish and believe her wish would come true. While her eyes were scanning the sky, she felt a wonderful fragrance from her right side that she had never felt before.

When she turned her head to that direction to figure out where it was coming from, the man who had just been shining with a glass in his hand in the far corner of the hall was standing opposite to her. He bowed, gave a very polite greeting without saying anything, and held out his right hand slowly to Maria.

He kissed her hand gently and asked, "Would you dance with me?"

Maria couldn't say anything. She just nodded with her head and smiled. She could not speak, as if she was drawn to the waters of a river flowing very strong. And she did not intend to make an effort to survive. The time for Maria seemed to stop again. She would not open her mouth because she felt like she would wake up from the dream. She was only staring into the young man's eyes. Together, they entered the hall and took a few more steps, leaving themselves to the rhythm of the music. The waters of the river calmed down. Under a clear sky, the river was slowly dragging the two towards the horizon, among large broad-leaved old trees lined up in two rows.

Maria suddenly asked, "Why?" And she immediately regretted as that was her first word.

The young man's smiling eyes shone even more. "Because you have a unique smile," he replied.

It was the first time that a man she had never met touched Maria. It wasn't like the touch of a dance teacher, brother or a relative. She felt she was starting to sweat. She was scared. Then she was pissed about their childish plan with her sisters. They tried to darken their skin by staying under the sun for a long time. So no one would like them.

She regretted this childish play. She wanted to be liked by the young man that she was dancing with. After a while, she started to look at the eyes which she was afraid to look at because she didn't know what to say. He had very deep blue eyes. They were pulling her like an irresistible, powerful vortex. She forgot she was dancing. Her feet and arms seemed to move independently of her. She just stared into the young man's eyes, smiling like him. She was happy.

63

Music stopped. They greeted each other. When Maria was asking the man for his full name, the other man which he was talking on the other side of the hall before, approached them. After a very respectful greeting to Maria, he turned to the young man and said, "It is time to go. They are waiting for us."

Maria was very excited. She didn't even know his name. The young man bent over and nodded, and then he kissed her hand. Maria didn't let go of the man's hand.

"What is your name? How can I ever see you again? Where do you live?"

She started to ask questions one after another. She had never tasted such beautiful emotions before, and the man, who was responsible for these feelings and whom she didn't know even his name was leaving. The young man approached Maria very calmly. Thinking that he would kiss her, Maria closed her eyes and began to wait for the moment when the young man's lips would touch her lips.

For the first time, a man was supposed to kiss her. The sisters had talked about how they would feel for years. She would find out soon. She thought that her heart rates could be noticed even from the outside. But she didn't care about anything anymore. The young man leaned in Maria's ear and said, "My name is Rua, my beautiful Princess. When you want to see me, just call my name. I'll come right away."

She was surprised that the young man didn't kiss her. At the same time, she was trying to keep in mind the young man's words. As the young man was moving away, she was thinking, "Rua? How is it written? How do I call him? Where does he live?."

She was asking questions like one after another again. She wanted to run after him and ask him these questions, but then she hesitated. She was afraid of the other people staring and laughing at her. She couldn't go after him.

64

"You made the wrong choice, Maria," she said to herself as hot water floated through her light brown hair pouring over her shoulders and covering her body. "You should have gone after him without minding anyone."

Then she continued to speak as if she was facing Rua.

"I called your name every day for months. You did not come. You didn't keep your promise."

The sound of water flow could have prevented those next to her from hearing, but someone who had seen her lips move could have thought she was out of her mind.

"But you're right, how would you come? How could you see me if you came?" said Maria and forgave the man she loved. You must have kept your word, I'm sure.

A single line of water flowing through her breast caught her attention. When they reached the protrusion of the navel, they split into two arms and went to separate paths to the right and left groin.

"That's how we broke up. Maybe someday we will pour into the same sea. Who knows?" Maria smiled.

Then she saddened again, "Would you accept a woman from a king's harem? Would you look at me the way you looked that night again? I looked for a soap that smelled like you. So I could wear you. I was sorry I couldn't find it at first but I'm glad that other girls will not be wearing you also."

The bathhouse suddenly became more enlightened. The clouds obscuring the sun had been gone. The sunrays started flowing through the holes in the dome. Maria looked at the dome and asked herself, "How long has it been since I've been free to wander under the sun? I don't think I can walk around anymore. Is that how my life will end? A gift to the king. Will my only purpose be to please him? What if he doesn't like me? Are they going to lock me up in the laundry like Gülnihal?"

In the meantime, the silver embroidery on her clogs caught her eyes. Then she looked at the bowl and the bow where she had water. They were all like a work of art, all made with great care. She had never seen similar patterns and embroidery before.

She thought of how harmonious everything was with each other. The door of the bath and even the bowl in her hand contained patterns that seemed to follow each other. She thought, if even the hammam was so beautiful, how would be the Sultan's room? Then she was afraid of her thought. She prayed that she would never see the Sultan's room.

65

"Finish your bathing and get dried. The physician woman is waiting for you!"

All the girls hurriedly got up from their stools. They began to dry by rubbing their loincloths to their bodies and hair.

The concubine said, "Come on. Leave everything in your hand, remove your loincloths, and stand by the wall!"

She pointed to the wall opposite the basins. They were stark naked again. "When will this torture end? We're like animals for sale," said Maria silently.

In the meantime, a physician came in with a large dark bag in her hand. First, she examined all the girls with her eyes only. Then she pointed to Maria and told her to wait at the back of the wall.

The physician passed behind the wall where girls were lined up. She told the concubine to send the girls one by one. First, she took the girl who Maria thought she was thirteen years old. There was no sound. Then, at the end of the wall, Maria saw the girl's left leg and realized that she was sitting and spreading her legs.

What kind of control is that? asked Maria herself. She occasionally heard low-pitched moans. At least she didn't scream. After the other two girls went through the same practice, it was Maria's turn. She went to the back of the wall with the concubine, albeit a little timidly. There was a stool as she had expected, but the physician did not want her to sit.

Starting with her neck, she examined her scalp and almost every strand of her hair. She then spread her arms and legs apart. Starting from her armpits, she examined Maria's entire body with her hands. She then told Maria to sit down. She re-examined her starting from her groin to the tips of her feet.

When Maria thought the examination was over, the physician told her to spread her legs thoroughly. Suddenly, the physician began to press down on Maria's vagina with her fingers. Maria began to look up the ceiling to avoid herself seeing what the Physician was doing. Then she realized that this time a thin and hard object was on her vagina and even a little inside.

As she reflexively threw herself back, the woman told her not to move, holding Maria's right leg firmly with her left hand. Maria didn't know what to do and what to say. Then she closed her eyes tightly and squeezed her teeth as much as possible. She started praying that the examination would end soon. She opened her eyes again after realizing that the object had been withdrawn. She saw the woman holding the stick to the spot where the light coming from the dome was brightest. She was examining it as if she was looking for a specific disease.

The physician turned to Maria and said, "Stand up and turn around."

Maria was sure that the Physician would focus on the scars on her body and ask questions about them. She started repeating the answers she had prepared earlier.

"Put your hands on the wall and spread your legs," said the woman. Maria was surprised that she wasn't interested in her scars. Maria did as the physician told so, wondering what the next command would be.

"More!" she said, shouting in a harsh voice. As Maria spread her legs a little further, she felt her fingers in her anus. She screamed and turned away.

"What are you trying to do? Am I an animal?" she shouted and pushed her away.

66

She fell down. Hearing the shouting, the concubine ran to them and slapped Maria. Then she shouted out loud to summon the other concubines. Maria was stunned for a moment by the impact of the hard slap she had. As Maria walked over to hit the woman back, her roommates stopped her.

Meanwhile, the hammam was filled with other concubines. Two of the concubines kicked Maria and laid her on the ground. They started to press on her back with their feet. In the meantime, the physician woman stood up and acted as if nothing had happened. Then she turned to the concubine who was responsible for the hammam and said that she wanted to finish the examination.

The concubines who laid Maria on the ground held her by the arms and leaned her against the wall. They hit her in the legs and forced her to open them wide. When the physician finished her examination, she asked Maria to turn her head. This time she thoroughly examined the scars on Maria's waist and legs and asked some questions.

Maria didn't answer. She was only staring with disgust at the physician and the concubine who slapped her. The concubine approached Maria and slapped her again.

"Answer her!"

Maria spat on her.

"This is my answer. I hope you liked it," she said. Then the concubines holding Maria by the arms laid her down again. The concubine placed a bowl on Maria's back and began to press with her foot.

"Look at me! I drown you in your saliva. It seems you haven't understood where you are. This bowl on your back is worth more than you. You'll remember that as you feel your pain," she said and kicked Maria's chin which was on the floor.

At that moment everyone in the hammam thought that Maria might be dead. The concubine, who has trained many girls who have caused problems in the harem for years, confidently turned to the other concubines.

"Put some clothes on her and send her to the dungeon."

Maria was lying on the floor with no sign of life.

67

Maria opened her eyes with an unbearable headache in a cell with her hands and feet chained. Her jaw ached so much that she couldn't even open her mouth. Her upper and lower teeth seemed to be intertwined. She thought that her jaw must be broken. She was afraid to check.

When she looked around with blurred eyes, she realized that she was in a dark cell. It was smaller than a square meter. The walls were covered with black stones. The ceiling was flat and there wasn't even a seat. As she felt a little bit better, she stood up and tried to get to know the cell better. But then, she gave up. She turned her face to the iron gate, leaned her back against the cold wall and sat down.

Her pain was increasing. She began to feel the pain on her wrists and back. "Don't think," she said to herself.

Then tears began to flow from her cheeks. "I was a princess just a few years ago. Look at me now."

She thought about the good times she spent with her family.

"I'm in a grave just like them. But alive. You can't escape from your destiny."

She heard footsteps from a distance. She thought that they were bringing water or something to eat. As the footsteps approached, she despaired and thought they were bringing another girl.

68

From her outfit and the two concubines standing behind her, Maria understood that she was a high-ranked concubine. After hitting the ground twice with the stick in her hand she said, "Get up!" in a very harsh tone. Maria didn't do what she said. She didn't even raise her head. She was sitting on the floor looking at a fixed spot as if there was no one else but her.

Then she looked up at the woman standing in front of her for a moment and closed her eyes. The high-ranked concubine ordered one of the girls to call the guard. A little while later, the guard opened the rusty iron gate and retreated. Two of the concubines entered and dragged Maria by her arms and threw her before the high-ranked concubine's feet.

"You have caused too much trouble from the first day. You must be thankful. You are forgiven by our holy Sultan. If it were up to me, I would take your life with my own hands."

Maria raised her head. She looked at the woman and smiled.

"I am already dead. How many times do you die? Looks like you've never tasted it. I can help you with that if you want."

The two young concubines and the guard, waited for the woman to be very angry and to teach Maria a good lesson. But she was standing quietly. They didn't understand whether she remembered her early days in the harem or whether she didn't want to spend more time with the ignorant girl. She walked away, telling the concubines who were standing on both sides of her, to bring Maria in her room.

69

Maria was standing on a wonderful Persian carpet, looking at her toes, without knowing what room she was in, as she was advised not to raise her head off the floor.

"Where did you come from?"

Maria recognized the voice. It was the voice of the high-ranked concubine who came to her cell. After a pause, Maria told the same story as she told to Gülnihal, silently. She waited for a sign of whether the woman believed her or not.

"You are lying," said the woman. "You're a good orator but a bad liar. How old are you?"

"Nineteen"

"You have very delicate hands for someone who is nineteen years old and has been cleaning ever since she knew herself."

Maria thought for a moment to tell her everything as it was and to ask her for help. Then she gave up believing that it wouldn't help. Besides, the man who brought her to Istanbul had urged her not to talk to anyone about anything. He would surely come and get her out of the Harem, Maria believed.

"But I am no longer in the house of Pasha. How will he find me?"

Maria despaired. Then she hoped that Pasha would send a message to the man who brought her to Istanbul.

While Maria was thinking of all of this, the concubine told her to get closer and sit down on the floor. When Maria had the chance to raise her head for the first time since she entered the room, she also tried to examine the room while walking. The walls were filled with beautiful calligraphy written in Arabic letters just like all over the palace. It was a very simply furnished room. The woman leaned her back on the back of the couch, sitting cross-legged and drinking something Maria had never seen before. But what surprised Maria was that they were alone in the room. However, she was a criminal, she was punished for attacking others.

"Does she think I'm harmless? There must be somebody else behind the doors," Maria thought. Then her outfit caught Maria's attention. Her outfit was more eye-catching than the outfit of the concubine in the kitchen. There were many different motifs embroidered on her dress with yellow threads. As the ranks rise, so does the clothes get better, she thought.

The concubine pointed to the place where Maria should seat when there was only a step distance between them.

"You don't look like other girls. What you did today could have cost you your life. Do you think death is just fainting? I will talk to you like a sister for a while. I want you to be relaxed. Our Sultan forgave your life. This is a great blessing. Don't worry. Nobody can hurt you despite his high word. But I need to know you too. So I ask you again. Where did you come from?"

70

"Who is the Sultan?" Maria thought to herself and then answered the concubine.

"I just told them all. Believe me. There's nothing else. I've been a cleaner since I've known myself."

"This is your home from now on. You can get out of here either in a coffin or when you get too old to serve. You better get used to your new life. If somehow you find a chance to give birth to a Prince, you may become the ruler of the Harem. If you use your mind, you can become a Hurrem Sultan or Kösem Sultan. But if you keep on causing troubles in the Harem, you will end up dead. You will determine your destiny. Stay out of sight for a while. I will send you to the laundry room. Don't forget what I said. Now go and get some sleep without saying anything to anyone. You will be attending classes tomorrow morning. And you will help Gülnihal in the afternoons. You do what she says. This is Harem. Here the wind changes quickly. It may not take a long time for our Sultan to change his mind."

Maria didn't know what to say or if she had to say something. When she wanted to stand up, she sat back because of the pain in her ankles.

"Can't I get out of here? I don't mean to bother anyone or cause any trouble. I just want to leave."

The concubine smiled slightly.

"You are the property of our Sultan. You can't go anywhere without his permission. Go ahead, go to bed."

Maria left the room constantly saying, "I am a property."

She began to walk towards the dormitory with the concubine waiting at the door.

71

A little ahead of the doorway, the mirrored door of the walnut cabinet was opened on the right-hand wall. A concubine came out of it and she walked over to the woman and stopped one meter before giving a very respectful salute by breaking her knees. There was a fancy dagger with precious stones attached to the belt wrapped around her waist.

"Pick one of her roommates. Tell her to spy on Maria. That girl will tell you every day what she does at nights, whether she speaks in her dream, if so, in which language and what she speaks, with whom she becomes a friend."

72

The concubine took Maria to the tailor. She went out after saying something to the tailor. The old tailor woman, who had light gray colored hair, examined Maria carefully. She didn't need to take Maria's measurements. Then she went through the door behind the counter and disappeared.

When Maria was alone in the room, she glanced at the colorful fabrics on the shelves. They were all very good quality fabrics. She didn't know what to do. Could she sit? Or was it forbidden?

She remembered the dress that her mother gave her on her 17th birthday. It was a white long dress. She looked like a swan. She remembered her mother's warm smile and her sisters' staring at her with admiration. As she stared at herself in the mirror, she heard a gunshot. Her white dress was covered in blood. She startled and stepped back in fear. She hit the counter behind her and fell to the ground. She sat still on the floor for a while. She returned to reality and stood up.

"I can't even imagine anymore."

Meanwhile, the old woman came in with clothes in her hand and said, "Come closer. You are going to wear these from now on. You will be given two dresses every year. If you want something else, you will have to buy it with your own money."

"With my own money? I don't have any money," said Maria surprisedly. The old woman looked at Maria for a moment with disgust and said, "Get out!"

73

Maria got out with her clothes in her hand and tried to find her way to the dormitory. The young concubine who brought her to the tailor wasn't in sight. She felt all alone in the palace. She looked at the large table made of walnut wood with candlesticks on it. It was in the middle of the large room.

Then she looked at the doors lined up in equal rows on the opposite wall. Everything seemed symmetrical. Only the colors disrupted that harmony. She noticed that the colors on both sides of the wall changed with a slight transition. When she looked at the paintings on the wall, she realized that the colors used on them were all in harmony with the basic colors of the walls.

She remembered a book she had read years ago about Asian Culture. Turks used to name each direction with a different color. The North was black. The South was white. The East was yellow. The West was red. The north was black because it was unknown. The south was white because it was known. The East was yellow because of the sunrise. The West was red because of the sunset. She understood that the colors hidden in the objects, walls, and paintings showed directions.

She wanted to go to her room and sleep without being seen. But she didn't know which way to go.

"I wish I would look around more carefully. I have to be more careful. Being locked is not a problem. The problem is not knowing how to get out," she said. She thought for a moment to go and ask the tailor. Then she gave up. She was afraid that the woman would shout at her again. She was scolded enough for one day. She turned to the right side where the yellow colors were predominant in the hall.

When she arrived at the end of the corridor, she couldn't decide which way to take. For a moment she remembered playing hide-and-seek with her sisters. She would win if she reached the castle without anyone seeing her. She heard some noises and stopped. She looked around, hoping to see someone she could ask the way to the dormitory, but she couldn't see anyone.

"Hello! I'm lost. How can I get to the dorm?"

There was nobody around.

After taking a few steps, she heard the noises again. As soon as she turned around, she saw someone approaching her with a string in her hand. Maria stepped back as the woman tried to strangle her. When the woman made another move to put the string around Maria's throat, another woman grabbed Maria's neck with both hands. They were trying to tear off Maria's necklaces and bracelets. Maria was barely breathing. She would either faint or die if they continue to strangle her.

74

"I can't take them off!"

"Use your knife"

Maria felt that she was fainting. She couldn't shout and ask for help.

"What's happening here?" All of a sudden, the hall lights turned on. When Maria barely opened her eyes and looked in the direction of the sound, she saw a group of women behind a man in uniform. There was a silence of death. Maria who was standing on her knees, couldn't stand any longer. She collapsed.

When the people in the room saw that Maria had her hands tied behind her back, their astonishment increased. The man in uniform turned to the woman on his left.

"Arrest them!"

Maria turned to the man and said, "Help me! They are trying to kill me!"

75

Two of the concubines lifted Maria. Maria was barely standing. After the struggle, which seemed to never end, she began to breathe comfortably. She noticed that the man in uniform looked more like a Prussian officer than a Turkish officer.

The woman standing next to the man was unlike any other woman she had ever seen in the Harem. It was obvious that she was a noblewoman. Maria thought that she must be his wife.

Meanwhile, the man in uniform was looking at Maria. With her battered outfit and hair and her neck which was full of abrasions, she was no longer even looking like a concubine. Noticing that the man was looking at her, she dropped her head and realized that her breasts were almost out. She tried to close it with her hands, but she did not succeed.

"Get her up! Have the physician examine her!" said the man in uniform.

Daye Kalfa leaned almost to the floor and said, "Certainly, my Şehzade."

"Şehzade? So he must be one of the sons of the Sultan. Why does he have a cross on him? Is he Christian?" asked Maria herself.

76

When Maria opened her eyes, she could see nothing. It was dark. She couldn't remember where she was for a long time. I hope I'm dead, Maria thought. Then the scent of ointment reminded her where she was. She was in the infirmary.

She needed to go to the bathroom. As she walked barely in the dark, she tried to open the first door she came across. It was locked. As Maria walked away, the door opened from the inside.

"Why are you up at this time? Go and sleep. You need to rest."

Maria couldn't see who she was speaking. But she sounded familiar.

"I need to go to the bathroom," she said.

"Go through the door in the middle of the wall behind you. Everything you need is there," said the woman standing at the door.

Maria noticed the familiar scent coming from the room, rather than her answer.

"Grigori Yefimovich Rasputin."

For a moment she thought that the man who had ruined their lives was inside the room. Wasn't he dead? Did they lie to us? She thought that even if he didn't die, he couldn't come to the Ottoman Palace and live in the same room as the Physician. Though it was widely known that he had an undeniable effect on women. This effect had caused his death. For a moment she believed that Rasputin was in the room with the Physician. She took a few steps back when she felt as though he would appear with his hypnotic eyes. She started thinking about what to do if she saw him.

"Don't be ridiculous, Maria! You're losing your mind. You are getting afraid of your own shadow. Calm down. This is not possible."

77

"This is the house of our Holy Sultan, the representative of God on earth, the ruler of the world. You are the concubines honored to serve him and his family.

To serve our Lord is to serve God. No matter what, you will not raise your voice. You do not have the right to get angry. If there is a situation to complain about, you will forward it to the guards. This palace has eyes. It sees. This palace has ears. It can hear. This palace can speak. Keep these in your minds, if you want to live."

Education had begun. Maria and her roommates would learn how to walk in the palace.

"Be quiet and invisible. The floor of the harem is slippery. If you don't know how to walk, you fall. You will take short and narrow steps. You will learn how to walk. All you have to do is to look less, to show less and to talk less. You will learn how to speak and understand without saying a word."

Maria had learned from an early age how important the body language was. She had long learned the methods of understanding the body language of the other person. Knowing all of this, though, could not help her or her family. They all thought their executioners were rescuers.

"It's not important to know. Can you practice what you've learned, under the fear of death? That's what is important," said Maria to herself.

78

After walking for hours without any break, girls stopped by the sign of Kalfa. When the concubine told the girls to go to the edge of the wall and have some rest, they thought that the torture was over. They threw themselves to the edge of the wall and collapsed.

Maria noticed that the little girl sitting next to her was crying. She leaned over to her left ear and said, "Stay strong. It will end soon."

"I don't want to stay strong. I want to die. I am sick of all this."

"How old are you?"

"Thirteen."

Maria thought for a moment what a thirteen-year-old girl might have had to wish to die. She recalled the days when she was stuck between committing suicide and staying alive to get revenge. Then she got angry with herself. There were many other options in life besides these two.

"Trust me. This place is much safer from the outside," said Maria.

"If there were a God, I wouldn't have gone through this. Either there is no God or he is only the God of some other people. I've never been a child. I've been bought and sold for as long as I can remember. I don't even know if I had a family. I can't walk the way they want. I am sure they are going to sell me again. I'm so bored. I'm so tired of living. It is enough."

She feared that what she had said might have been heard. She looked around and stuck her head between her knees again.

"God hasn't left you since you are still alive. We die when we sleep and we born when we wake up again everyday. You never know what life will bring you. Sometimes it only takes a few seconds to become a slave from a princess. Not every princess dies as a princess, and not every slave has to die as a slave," said Maria.

The young girl turned to Maria and said, "I have to talk to you tonight."

79

After taking lessons about palace etiquette all day, they allowed Maria to go to the infirmary. As she passed through the small hall leading to the infirmary, she saw a large mirror with silver frames adorned with unique embroidery hanging on the wall. She hesitated at first. Then she began to examine her face carefully. She hoped to see the traces of her family in her face.

"I'm ashamed to survive."

"So you started talking with the mirrors?" Maria heard a loud laugh after these words. She felt as if she had been caught committing a crime.

"Gülnihal?"

"Yes, it is me, Gülnihal. I didn't know it would make you so happy to see me."

Maria embraced her tightly. "Yes, I'm so happy to see you." At that moment, the arms of Gülnihal were the safest place for Maria in the world. Although Maria's initial reaction surprised Gülnihal, she could understand it. She knew what Maria was going through. There was nothing more valuable in the Harem than having a trusted friend.

"Don't be sad. They must be proud of you for holding on to life," said Gulnihal.

While they were walking towards the infirmary, Maria had dozens of questions in her mind. She knew that Gulnihal was the only one she could ask, but she was very uncertain about whether to ask her. She remembered her father's advice.

"If something stops you from doing something about what you want to do, don't do it. Either it's not the right time, or it's not the right thing to do."

80

Maria's treatment was over. Gülnihal directed Maria to a small room. It was a very small room. It was only three steps long from wall to wall. But starting from the ceiling, it was full of unique decorations. The ceiling was almost like a large painting. At its center was an eight-pointed star and a forest made of tree motifs surrounding it. It was consist of seven rings arranged one after the other in a circle. When she looked at the corners of the ceiling more carefully, she saw that they were all painted in different colors with depictions of trees.

Four different types of trees reminded her of the seasons. On further examination, she understood that they were not only showing the seasons, but also the directions. In a corner, there was a white tree without leaves on a black background. "This palace is certainly speaking," said Maria. She heard Gulnihal's voice as she slid her eyes down to understand what else the walls were saying.

"You're dreaming again. Are you in love? Come on, follow me."

"Wine. It makes you forget what you want to forget. It reminds you of what you want to remember. Taste it, Maria. This wine is 600 years old. Each drop is distilled from the bodies of concubines. It is our blood that gives this wine its red color. It doesn't lie. It reveals the perpetrator immediately. Come on, join your sisters now," said Gülnihal and held out a chalice towards Maria.

"You have become a real concubine."

Maria went to bed quietly, trying not to wake anyone.

81

"Can we talk?"

…

"Thank you for helping me today. I wouldn't have survived without you. I want you to know. They assigned me to spy on you. They asked me to tell them who you talked to at night, where you went, what you did, every day."

Maria smiled at her and said, "Then don't worry. Your job won't be too hard. I'm going to do laundry every day."

Maria stayed in the Harem until October 11, 1922.

82

Paris, 26 June 2017

As in the morning of June 26th each year, Adige awakened with excitement in her spacious apartment which was overlooking the Alexander III Bridge built by her grandfathers. As every June 26, she watched people crossing the bridge. Some fussy, and some calm.

"Happy Birthday Grandma."

After breakfast, she took her grandmother's diary and opened the section where her grandmother had written about Harem and the old concubine, who helped her to reunite with the man she loved.

83

Topkapı Palace, Istanbul, 11 October 1922

Various rumors were in circulation in the harem about Sultan's escape from the country. Even though the officials in the Harem said that the Sultan could never abandon the Capital city, everyone knew that the Sultan was preparing to leave.

This morning, they sent a total of seven concubines together with me and my best friend Gülnihal, to Topkapı Palace. It was known as the old palace. We were going to collect some of the personal belongings of Sultan Vahdettin and his family.

Although I had been in Istanbul for about four years, I was going out for the first time. I've never seen any place other than Harem and the Pasha's house.

In the years of the occupation, news about the suffering of the people and the atrocities of the allied soldiers would come to the Harem.

Against these atrocities, it was said that the Turkish youth were organized among themselves and even once they kidnapped a British officer. They took him to a hammam in Sarıyer, beat him first, and then raped him.

We got into a horse carriage. Nobody was talking. After a straight path, we started to descend a steep hill. In the meantime, as far as I can see from the caged window, we should have come out of the palace. There were houses made of wood. Unlike the rumors in the Harem, there were no British or Greek soldiers. People were looking contented.

"What has been said must be true. The golden man has won."

Mustafa Kemal Pasha's name in the Harem was the golden man. They couldn't call him with his real name as they thought that Sultan Vahdettin would be furious. Everyone in the Harem tried to follow his struggle against the occupation forces and prayed for his success.

84

The horse cart stopped shortly after the Imperial Gate. While silence was going on, I noticed that Gülnihal was staring fixedly at a point on the right, in a sad and pensive way. Then I heard her saying, "Hangman's Fountain."

"If the Valide Sultan had not forgiven me and sent me to the laundry room after the fight in the Harem, the executioners who would cut my head would wash their swords and hands in this fountain."

After the carriage went a little further, it stopped again in front of the Harem entrance gate in the second courtyard. We got out of the carriage with the call of one of the masters. They ordered us to line up in front of the gate.

After a while, the ant nest at the end of her foot caught the attention of Gülnihal. The ants were carrying something frantically into their nests. Gülnihal turned to me and said, "Maybe we are the ants of others."

I didn't understand what Gülnihal meant.

She continued, "Are we as important as we think in this big universe?" Gülnihal had read a lot of books although she was a concubine.

Then, she pointed the marble columns which were standing at the entrance of the third courtyard.

"Those are the columns I told you about," she said with a smile.

Gülnihal had previously told me that those columns were etched by Baltacılar.

"How is it be possible for the concubines to meet with them?" I asked in surprise.

"I told you before. You can never guess whom a concubine can know. You put a young girl among hundreds of other girls and keep them in Harem for years. What are you waiting for? They would do anything to escape. They believe that Baltacılar could help them. They flirt with these men in order to escape from the Harem. Later, I will show you the girls' writings on the walls."

Gülnihal pointed out the entrance of the palace doors and continued, "Look, every entrance in this palace is flat, without any entrance stairs. But on the other hand at the new palaces like Dolmabahçe and Yıldız, you have to climb a lot of stairs to enter them. As the palace gates became higher, the power of the empire got lower."

We entered the Harem. An old woman greeted us. The old woman gave all the girls their tasks. She told me "You're coming with me."

85

We were left alone in a small room. It was obvious that she was a beautiful woman long ago. She had long straight hair, delicate hands, smooth facial features, and the most beautiful blue eyes I have ever seen.

"You know, now you are a candidate to be a Valide Sultan," she said.

I didn't know if she knew that I was pregnant. I couldn't decide whether I could trust this woman or not. That's why I kept my silence. The man who rescued me and my brother told me to never speak with anyone unless it was a life and death situation. He promised he would come and take me home after the war. But I didn't have a home anymore. It has been four years, and nobody appeared.

"There's a lot you need to know about the harem. Follow me. Don't ask too many questions. Just listen."

When she started walking, my amazement was replaced with fear. I thought I came here to carry goods. Now the old woman in front of me was saying that she would tell me about Harem. Gülnihal had told me all about Harem before. What could I have not known? While I was thinking of being in a trap again, I checked the dagger with my hand which was hidden under my skirt. How much trouble could this old woman cause to me?

86

Istanbul was the capital city of the greatest Islamic Empire the world has ever known in the sixteenth century and it was ruled by Sultan Süleyman Khan. But actually, this isn't true. Because it has never been ruled according to Holy Kuran. Its zenith point was the period of Sultan Mehmet the second. After his death, the empire began to decline.

In the Ottoman Empire, the center of power was Topkapı Palace for many centuries. And the Harem was the heart of Topkapı Palace. Hundreds of women from all over the Empire came to Harem.

In 1520, a newcomer, named Alexandra Lisowska, came to Harem. She was coming from Ukraine. Her dad was a priest. She was brought to Harem by slave hunters and was given in the service of Sultan Süleyman.

The Allegretto of Joseph Hyden's Symphony No. 63 is known as La Roxelane.

Roxelane is the name of Hurrem Sultan in the western world. La Roxelane is actually the second part of the symphony. The Ottoman Empire, on the one hand, has been a source of inspiration for western artists with their rituals, music and palace figures. Inspired by Hurrem Sultan, Hyden named the second part of his symphony as La Roxelane. After that, the symphony was called Roxelane.

Turks cannot be enslaved in Ottoman Empire because Kuran was forbidding the enslavement of freeborn Muslims. Slavs or Caucasus women were usually captured for their white skin, dark hair and delicate bone structure. They were predominantly Christian.

You know, writing about the harem and the sultan's women or talking about them is a sin and it is forbidden. So nobody has written anything and people always have to decorate these stories in their imagination and foreign travelers have also done this.

People were very taken with the idea that we were all locked up together in a small house. They soon came up with fictitious stories about the harem. Most of those stories involved lots of sex and a lot of rather abusive treatment of young women.

The first man, besides the Sultan himself and the eunuchs who entered and saw the Harem was an English mechanic. He was sent by Queen Elizabeth the first to the palace of the great Sultan to install her gift of an organ.

He wrote,

'Through the grate, I did see 30 of the grand señores concubines who were playing with a ball. At first sight, I thought they'd been young men. But when I saw the hair of their heads hanging down on their backs, I didn't know them to be women and very pretty ones indeed. They wore breeches so thin I could discern the skin of their thighs good. I stood so long looking upon them that he who had shown me began to be very angry and stamped with his staff to make me give overlooking.'

87

Harem was the center of felicity. As Sultan had a special relationship with God, all the means of happiness were supplied to Harem. The best food, the best things to drink, the best music, the best singing, the best manuscripts with figures in them which are frowned upon by straight Muslims.

In Harem, when the girls first arrive, they would be examined to make sure that they didn't have any physical defects and any diseases.

I remembered my first physical examination in the bathhouse. I felt so humiliated. I pushed the physician to stop her. And then one of the servants in the bath knocked me down and kicked me in the head. I had fainted. I wondered, why this old woman was telling me all the things I know, the events I've been through.

88

Women come to the harem at an early age. And as soon as they arrive their clothes are changed and they're taken directly to the Hammam. They are cleaned according to traditions and taught how to wash before prayer. The type that Turkish men like is called flesh firm like a fish. And another detail, the belly should be shaped like a quince. In Turkish literature, when they describe women, they say cheeks like peaches, lips like cherries, similes like these and that's what men expect.

Islamic religious law permits polygamy. A man could marry up to four women at any given time. And he could also have concubines on the other side. But the numbers of polygamous marriages were very few. Only the ruling class for example like the Sultans and the Pashas and some rich men would have a harem. Moreover, the Harem is not only an Ottoman institution. It was also in the pre-Ottoman states. There were harems in Rome, Ancient, Greece and Aztec and all over China. All the ancient civilizations had a harem.

When Sultan Süleyman Khan was a young ruler, it was said that he was very lustful. He frequently visited the palace of the women. And indeed the Sultan was encouraged to behave a bit like a prize stud to cover more and more so that the biological future of the dynasty was secured.

The reason that the Ottomans chose to reproduce through concubines is that it gave them more reproductive freedom. The difference between having a child from a concubine and having a child from let's say a royal princess is that the princess as a married woman would have many more rights as a mother. Concubines, as they are slaves, have fewer rights over children.

The Sultan was considered to be above society and he was separated from it. That was the main ideology of the state. You can imagine that a relationship by marriage to a free Muslim woman, some would immediately make the Sultan related to a segment of society and this may cause divisions with other segments of society. The Ottomans did not take girls from the noble Turks in their own country and do not want them to rise as a force against them. That's why they prefer concubines.

Concubines are the personal slaves of the Sultans. They don't have any family and they don't have any connections.

89

At that moment my memories rose in revolt against her words. I am not a slave. My family's armies have shaken the walls of these palaces for hundreds of years.

You know the feelings of the women who entered the harem. Fear and insecurity as well as other emotions. But also the delight of material comforts. And there was the possibility of becoming the Sultan's consort.

In the sixteenth century, Istanbul had one of the most secret societies in the world, especially in the Imperial harem. Even today it is difficult to discover precisely what is going on here. People have always asked questions to women who left harem, and they are still asking. As it was prohibited to talk about life in the Harem, they could tell nothing. That's why the stories about Harem don't go beyond the old Western fantasies.

We should think of the Harem as a unique place as a collection of females who were more highly educated and trained in a variety of ways than women in the general society. So I think we might think of the Imperial harem as the only female University in the Empire.

The most important undergraduate was the priest's daughter Alexandra now known as Hurrem, meaning the laughing one.

When a woman like Hurrem arrived in the harem she would be given further education and by education I mean some religious training, knowledge of Islam. She would be taught the etiquette of the court. She would be trained in the skill that most harem women were adept at.

That is embroidery. Wonderful things. The embroidery that she produced could be sold through agents on the market.

So it was a profitable skill. It wasn't just a gentlewomanly skill.

They learned the Palace attitude. That was not very easy. How to greet people and to walk backwards to leave the Sultan's room. And how to be respectful and well-behaved at all times and never be angry.

They had lessons every day and most learned to read and write and to read the Koran.

Had the prying eyes of Western travelers pierced the outer walls they would have perceived a vastly different harem from the sexual paradise or inferno of their imagining.

Making love is the one thing most inmates of the harem were not doing at least if they were following the rules. Relatively a few of them got to spend the night with the Sultan. Living here was very claustrophobic for some, if you got a relatively small space with several hundred women living in it. Access to the outside world is very limited.

The views over Istanbul if you could get them, must have been, had quite an effect on people. It was a very comfortable place but it was more like a comfy prison than a comfy bordello.

And the prison warders were the eunuchs. They were the only men, who had been castrated, were allowed into the harem regularly. And just like the women, most eunuchs would spend their entire lives here.

The enclosure of women itself seems very objectionable. Perhaps even more objectionable is the mutilation of young men in order to provide eunuchs to staff and protect the harem.

It was forbidden by Islamic law to castrate a Muslim or perform the operation on others. So it was carried out by Coptic Christian priests in Egypt.

There are two methods of castration. One is cutting the testicles and other twisting and crushing them.

Eunuchs kept silver quills in their turbans. They would use those quills in order to urinate. But it was also a weapon. A needle with poison was on its tip.

One of the duties of the eunuchs was to ensure that the concubines did not have sex with anyone but the Sultan.

Cucumbers were not let into the harem unless chopped. Because they were used as a penis.

But the guards themselves will not be on suspicion.

The process of castration was very frightening and difficult for the boys. And often out of fear, their testicles would retreat.

They would remain intact and sometimes over time they would be able to function sexually. Ali Pasha, who died in the war in Peter Varadin in 1716, forbade castrating. He said, it wasn't humanitarian. However, after he died, the castration process continued.

90

In the early days, the Eunuchs were white slaves of Greek or Bosnian origin. The management of the harem was under the control of these eunuchs. From the end of the sixteenth century, they were replaced by black eunuchs from Nigeria and Chad. There are many accounts of the eunuchs having relationships with the women in the harem. This was one of the reasons why the eunuchs in the harem were exclusively African after the end of the sixteenth century.

It was one way of making sure that these men couldn't inseminate the female members of the Imperial family without everybody noting that she had given birth to a half-black child.

But for Hurrem as for most newcomers to the harem, there was little opportunity for a dalliance with eunuchs or anyone.

If the girls were higher in the power structure of the harem, they would be given their own quarters. But the rest of the girls would share their rooms. There were older women who watched over the younger girls to make sure that they weren't getting into any kind of mischief. Such as talking in the dark, sharing their bed.

It was not perhaps for the happiest of estates for the daughter of the Priest. But if Hurrem dreamed of improving her lot, there was always the possibility of sex with the Sultan. Though this too was hedged with its own barriers of ritual and restraint.

Some of the Sultans like to watch lots of pretty girls sort of dancing all together. Sultan would throw a handkerchief towards the woman who caught his eye.

The surprised virgin snatches of this prize and good fortune with such eagerness that she is ravished with joy before she is deflowered by the Sultan. For most harem women not yet numbered among the favorites, a handkerchief was just another item of laundry.

Very few of them ever got to see the Sultan. And let alone jump into his bed. You had to maneuver yourself into position with the women who chose who went to bed with the Sultan, especially his mother.

In reality, the Sultan's mother would scout for suitable candidates among these now derelict pools and fountains in the bowels of Topkapı. And the physical attraction was far from being her only criteria.

An eligible concubine would obviously need to be attractive. She needed to be healthy. Because her principal job was reproduction. Because of the important role that mothers played in training their sons, she also needed to be shrewd.

And the way they were introduced was that they were asked to go to a pool underneath the Crown Princess apartment.

And that was an opportunity for the Sultans to watch and observe them and choose their favorite.

Although İbrahim Pasha brought Hurrem to the attention of the Sultan or indeed his mother, the preparations for her first night with him would have followed a well-established ritual.

The day she is going to be with the Sultan, she goes to the bathhouse and has face and body treatments. And her hands and hair are painted with henna.

The idea of any hair on the body was thought of horror and so they would remove any kind of hair including their pubic hair. What they used was really an awful smelling paste that contained arsenic. And if you left it too long, it could burn the skin very badly. And they used mussel shells to scrape it off. They would put henna four fingers above the pubic area. It's a decorative beautiful design detail.

91

When the old woman mentioned the paste, I remembered of the paste that Gülnihal and her friends used in the Turkish bath. But these putties were not for cleansing the body. They made them into joyous substances with various herbs.

Concubines are assumed to be virgins. But I don't think we can assume the naivete and the innocence that kind of goes along with the whole notion of virgins. I mean these women were prepared for their job.

All the older women and those who have had his good graces before going to the favorite of the day congratulating her for the great distinction which she has received. And saluting her as befits the concubine of the Emperor dressing her superbly and taking her out with countless jewels. She would be given new clothes and shoes and trained also in the erotic arts.

I was so embarrassed when I left the Prince's room. I couldn't get my eyes up from the floor until I went to the bathhouse with the concubines waiting outside the door. On the following day, the gifts sent by the Prince caused me to feel worse.

92

The Sultan's mother, his sisters, experienced women, high-level women within the harem would provide the finishing touches. They would explain a particular person that the concubine would encounter.

A concubine must enter the bed from the foot of the bed so the Sultan would be waiting for this beauty to crawl from the foot of the bed and reach him.

Whatever happened that night, Sultan Suleyman wanted it to continue. Hurrem was invited back to his bed again and again. She was soon firmly established as the Sultan's favorite. Sultan Suleyman excluded the other concubines. He fell in love with her.

A deadly rivalry had reached into the harem. It was not simply a question of who would occupy the Sultan's bed. It was a far more vital conflict over who would produce the next ruler of the Ottoman Empire. The new favorite Hurrem or the old favourite Mahidevran.

Mahidevran was the mother of the oldest son. So that Hurrem coming in obviously being the Sultan's new favorite was a threat to her.

Hurrem Sultan made a very wise plan. One day, Hurrem Sultan made threatening gestures undisguisedly; then arose such angry mutterings that Mahidevran Sultan could not be deaf to them.

Mahidevran picked a fight with Hurrem and called her, soiled meat. A piece of meat off the slave market. And this provoked a physical struggle between them. Hurrem's face was scratched, her hair was pulled.

And the next time the Sultan called for Hurrem, she replied she was unworthy of his attention since she was soiled meat. The Sultan ordered Hurrem to come to his room again. Her face was scratched and her head was scattered. When he asked, Hurrem Sultan said that your concubine, Mahidevran, made that to her. After that, Mahidevran was sent from the Palace to Manisa near his son Şehzade Mustafa as an exile.

Thus, Istanbul was completely in the hands of Hurrem Sultan.

This was an early sign of Hurrem's intelligence and ability to manipulate the whole palace system. Hurrem knew how to play her cards.

You have to think about how these women achieved what they wanted. It was incredibly a bit intensely sort of concentrated intrigue. They were battling for a position to produce an heir.

93

Hurrem gave birth to her first son Prince Mehmet in 1521. If Sultan Suleyman had played the game by the rules, he should now have moved on to a new woman. But he didn't.

Before Hurrem's time, if a concubine of the Sultan gave birth to a son then she was kicked out of his bed. Hurrem produced one son but then she gave birth to several more. Suleyman kept her in his bed.

There are many reasons for one mother and one son principle. Mothers are important advisors to their sons. Two sons sharing a mother meant they only had half of an advisor and half support. If a woman is identified with only one son, she is completely with him in this game of power. And it was a game Hurrem had to win. Under Islamic law, all sons had an equal right to inheritance. But in the Ottoman Court, the losers lost more than the throne.

Sons of a Sultan were in combat. Survival of the fittest, the one who was the strongest, the ablest became the Sultan.

The sons were going to vie amongst themselves to become the Sultan. And it was winner-take-all. They had to race to Constantinople, they had to raise the support and when they became Sultan, they put all their brothers to death.

All dynasties have had a problem in securing an uninterrupted and legitimate succession. Many wars have been started in England and France by discontented royal brothers or cousins or other relations. The Ottoman solution was to have a harem with no lack of a male heir. After the Sultan's succession, other male members of the dynasty were murdered.

By 1530 Süleyman had five sons and four of them were by Hurrem.

94

Hurrem troubled people. They weren't used to a Sultan keeping up a relationship with one woman. And they worried that Suleyman had gone head over heels in love. People even went so far as to call her a witch. Because of their fear that she had somehow seduced the Sultan.

New concubines were brought into the harem in the hope of tempting Suleyman from the path of fidelity. They included two Russian women with the same highly-prized looks as Hurrem. Women given directly to the Sultan would be highly cultivated, attractive, intelligent women. Naturally, Hurrem saw a competition. So here we see another sign of Hurrem being able to manipulate the politics of the Harem and to use her own special position as a real favorite of the Sultan. She ruled them out with little mind games with her intelligence. She made them get married before they even met the Sultan.

And then in 1534, fourteen years after Suleyman and Hurrem first made love, the Sultan made an even bigger break with tradition.

There occurred the most extraordinary event. Unprecedented in the history of the Sultans. Süleyman has taken Hurrem to himself at his Empress. A slave woman from Russia.

He married her. It was an incredible thing. Sultans didn't marry their concubines. They didn't need to.

The concubine by definition is a man's female slave. According to religious law, you can't marry your own concubine. So you have to free her in order to marry her.

Hurrem used her famous intelligence here as well. One day, she told Sultan Suleyman that she wanted to donate to Kabe. Sultan Süleyman welcomed this. But Sultan had missed a point. Slaves could not donate to Kabe. Then he gave her freedom. Hurrem then donated to Kabe. On one of the following days, he called Hurrem. She replied that she was now a free woman, without being married, she couldn't be with him. It would be a sin. After that, they got married.

One thing it meant was power. For the first time in their history, the Ottomans had a queen.

After she was married, we started calling her Hurrem Sultan. And she was really like a Queen. She built up diplomatic relations, and she also influenced her husband politically.

The Harem was not in the Topkapı Palace. It was in the palace called the palace of tears in Beyazıt. Hurrem has also moved Harem into the Topkapı Palace. Thus, she could better control Sultan Suleyman and the political climate.

But for long periods the two lovers were apart. Süleyman was a fighting Sultan who had already extended his empire westward.

Süleyman took Belgrade. He destroyed the whole of the Hungarian ruling classes in 1526 in the battle of Mohaç. At a stroke and rode into Buda, a conqueror. And by 1529 he was at the gates of Vienna.

But even on the campaign, his thoughts were with Hurrem. He sent frequent love letters and poems.

I will read you some examples of poems and the letters that they sent to each other during campaigns.

'The green of my garden, my sweet sugar, my treasure, my love who cares for nothing in this world. My master of Egypt, my Joseph, my everything. The queen of my hearts Rome. My land of the Roman Caesars my Baghdad and Khorasan.'

'If the seas were to become ink and these trees pens. When could they write an account of this parting? There is no limit to the burning anguish of separation. Let my soul gain at least some comfort from a letter. Your son and daughter weep from missing you.'

But Hurrem's letters also reveal her fears for the safety of her sons. The favored heir to the throne was Prince Mustafa.

The son of Hurrem's old rival Mahidevran. Mustafa had the support of the army and the Grand Vizier İbrahim Pasha. Some viziers were captured slaves like İbrahim Pasha. He did become a companion and a favorite of the Sultan. They would generally dine together and his bed was in the same room as the Sultan's bed.

So as a very young man in his twenties, he was suddenly the top man in the Empire after the Sultan himself.

95

People today still say that Sultan Suleyman had cemented this relationship by giving his own sister in marriage to Ibrahim. In reality, it was İskender Pasha, who was the husband of Sultan Süleyman's sister. They had a son. His name was Osman Shah. The name of İbrahim Pasha's wife was Muhnise. They had a son named Mehmet Shah.

Ibrahim Pasha's wedding was very showy, continued for many days. As Sultan Süleyman personally came to the wedding, stayed one night and paid all the costs, it was considered as a Sultan's wedding by society. This is totally wrong.

İbrahim's prestige was something Hürrem could not tolerate. We should not forget that we are talking about power politics here. Sixteenth century Ottoman Empire was at its height. That meant tremendous power. So, of course, she wanted to undermine him.

In one of her letters, Hurrem referred to a disagreement with Ibrahim Pasha. She wrote to Suleyman.

'And now you inquire about why I'm not with Ibrahim Pasha. You'll hear about it when I am granted my next meeting with you. For the moment give the Pasha our greetings. We hope they will be acceptable to him.'

İbrahim Pasha acquired lots of wealth within a very short time. Süleyman the Magnificent could figure out where that wealth was coming from. At least partially it was bribery. If bribe and corruption were among İbrahim's faults, another was an arrogant assumption of his own worth.

He was once quoted as saying, *'Though I am the Sultan's slave, whatsoever I declare is done. I can at a stroke make a Pasha out of a stable-boy. I can give kingdoms and provinces to whomsoever I choose and my Lord will say nothing against it. Even if he has ordered a thing himself, if I do not want it, it is not done. And if I order a thing to be done and he has ordered to the contrary, what I wish and not what he wishes is done.'*

And on the 15th of March 1536, İbrahim Pasha accepted the Sultan's invitation to dine with him. They ate at the same table until late at night according to Ramadan traditions. They talked and entertained themselves, and then they went to bed.

96

We don't really know what happened that night. But obviously, the Sultan had decided that the Grand Vizier had become too powerful.

As a complement to his boyhood friend Suleyman apparently ordered the same method of execution reserved for his own kin. Strangling with his own bowstring. So there would be no spilling of royal blood. But İbrahim put up too much of a struggle.

Sultan Süleyman was a man of iron. Anything that threatened the state or that threatened his own integrity as a ruler would motivate him to take violent moves.

İbraham's body was immediately taken out of the Topkapı Gate, which gave its name to Topkapı Palace, without any religious rituals. He was buried in the garden of Canfeda Tekke.

However, one of the gravediggers who loved the Pasha very much, planted a hackberry tree at least to make sure that the burial place was certain. That tree still stands there.

This is a reminder of how the Ottoman government worked. You could raise a peasant from the dust to be a Grand Vizier but his life hung by a thread.

The next day, all the properties of İbrahim were confiscated, and his wife and children were taken out of their palace. No more news from the Pasha's family was heard.

It's hard to see that Süleyman himself would have done it without Hurrem. She wanted to be absolutely sure of her control. And until İbrahim was out of the way there was always a danger that she might be packed off herself. She was ruthless. She had to be ruthless.

But the danger remained. And death was not under Hurrem's exclusive control.

97

In 1543 Hurrem's ambitions received a fatal blow. Her young son Prince Mehmet was struck down by smallpox. His death began a new race for the succession and the front-runner was Mustafa, who was the son of Hurrem's old rival, Mahidevran and now in his late thirties.

This would mean death for Hurrem's surviving sons.

Sultan Süleyman's favorite son was known as Şehzade Mustafa. In fact, he saw Mehmet as his heir. When Mehmet died, Sultan Suleyman made the order for his son to be buried in the graveyard that he prepared for himself. Also, he placed a throne on Mehmet's shrine.

If Mustafa were to ascend the throne, the murder of her own children would be inevitable for Hurrem.

The story is usually looked at as one of intrigue and competition among the mothers around their sons. I think there's a larger political context for this. Mustafa was very popular with the soldiers.

He was a rival to his father without his meaning to be. Just by virtue of his popularity. And the Sultan was persuaded that Mustafa was conspiring against him.

The story is that Hurrem had an ally. Hurrem Sultan was such a smart woman that she, on the one hand, prepared her sons for the throne, and on the other hand, married her daughter Mihrimah to the famous Grand Vizier Rüstem Pasha. In this way, she took her power from Grand Vizier also.

The marriage of Rüstem Pasha to Mihrimah also has a story. According to the old belief, if a man is a leper or a leprosy patient, then there will be no louse on him. When he was going to marry Mihrimah, they rumored that Rüstem Pasha was a leper.

Pasha served in Diyarbakır at that time. Someday when he went to the bathhouse, a physician checked his clothes for louse. This was a physician who was assigned to Diyarbakır specifically for this task. He found a louse in his clothes. But the strange thing is that the second most powerful man in the empire has louse.

Though those who know Rüstem Pasha well, believe that after the rumors, he may have put the lice on his own. He was known for his intelligence. There are also many stories and narratives about how he rises.

Harem women could establish important alliances with male political actors to the marriages of their daughters. And this daughter's husband was the Grand Vizier.

The new Grand Vizier was an important ally for Hürrem. And ideally placed to whisper slanders in the Sultan's ear.

Word began to reach Süleyman while he was out on campaign that Mustafa was plotting against him. And Mustafa himself was very upset when news of these allegations reached him and he went to see his father.

And with the help of Rüstem Pasha, they accused Şehzade Mustafa of correspondence with the ruler of the Safavid Empire, of agreeing with him, of trying to replace his father.

98

Mustafa reached Suleyman's base in Iran. Before meeting his father, some janissaries cut his way and warned him not to go. However, Prince could not resist the Sultan's order. Also,

Mustafa did not believe that he had done something wrong, that his father would take his life.

The night before the meeting with his father, when he was in his camp, an arrow with a note was thrown onto Mustafa's tent. It was written on the note that he would be killed if he went to meet his father.

The next day, Mustafa went straight to his father's tent. As soon as he entered the tent, Sultan Süleyman said that Mustafa had betrayed him. Mustafa rejected this accusation, and deaf and mute executioners of the Sultan made a determined attack upon him.

They hurled Mustafa to the ground throwing a bowstring around his neck. Suleyman urged the executioners to greater efforts. But Mustafa succeeded to escape from the men. As he was running towards the exit of the tent, he fell to the ground with the tackle of Zal Mahmut Pasha.

Meanwhile, the executioners caught up and strangled him. Zal Mustafa Pasha was the husband of Hürrem Sultan's other daughter, Shah Sultan.

The janissaries, who had held Rüstem Pasha responsible for the death of Prince Mustafa, took action to kill him. Sultan Süleyman sent Rüstem Pasha secretly from the headquarter. When the anger of the Janissary did not stop, Rüstem Pasha was dismissed from his duty. He was replaced by Ahmet Pasha.

99

Two years later, Hürrem Sultan had him executed. Rüstem Pasha was again Grand Vizier instead. After the death of

Mustafa, Sultan Suleyman did not return to Istanbul for two years. Hürrem was widely blamed for her role in the murder. Süleyman and Hürrem had another son, named Cihangir. He was a humpback. He could not survive the psychological crisis after Mustafa's death. And he died forty days after Mustafa's death. This was the second child loss of Hürrem. I don't think Süleyman would have listened to these stories. If he hadn't himself felt that there was a legitimate threat. Despite the fact that he was going to alienate so many people by executing his son that this was probably the wiser move for the integrity of the Empire.

If tradition paints Hürrem as the villain of the piece it was at a time when powerful women were widely perceived as a threat to the established order. Hürrem's contemporaries were Queen Elizabeth of England, Catherine de Medici of France and Mary Queen of Scots whom the Calvinist John Locke's dubbed the monstrous regimen. Hürrem aroused similar hostility among the Ottoman elite, though the extent of her power has been disputed.

Hürrem was obviously a very powerful woman. It is difficult for us to know how powerful because of course, you know as today in the corridors of power, things are decided in corridors not written down. She was his eyes and ears and of course, when the Sultan is away it means she could probably do a few things on her own account as well.

Hürrem was a very smart and shrewd person. And she would write giving him news of what was going both within the family but also political news. There is one letter she wrote when Süleyman was fighting the Iranians.

She said, '*So everybody here in Istanbul is waiting for your good news. They're ready to set up a parade, and we don't have any good news from you. You need a victory. Now if a messenger arrives saying no progress here nothing there. No one is going to be very happy, my Sultan.'*

Hürrem was sensitive to public opinion, and she embarked on an ambitious building plan.

One of the major expressions of power was building large mosques. That had in the prerogative of males in the dynasty. And Hürrem is in some ways the first woman who builds quite publicly.

But the public expression of Hürrem's power was undermined by a fatal flaw. She had removed the main rival for the throne but she had two sons and they couldn't both rule. Under Ottoman law, one of them would have to die. Before the problem could be resolved, she became seriously ill. Suleyman was old then and also in bad health kept vigil at her bedside. But even as he watched her fight for life, he must have known he would have to make a terrible choice over which of their sons would succeed him.

It was probably Hürrem's fortune that she did not live long enough to see the power struggle between her two sons. The younger son took arms against his older brother and the Sultan.

Süleyman had his youngest son executed as a traitor. But by then he had lost the love of his life. Hürrem died on April the 18th, 1558. Thirty-eight years after she had first entered the harem.

Eight years after Hürrem's death, Süleyman joined her in the cemetery of Süleymaniye Mosque.

Although she was unpopular at that time, Hürrem built the foundation of this very public power that women had. Her power as a concubine troubled many people. A sexually active woman in power was a problem.

Hürrem had devoted 38 years of her life to ensuring that one of her sons succeeded to the throne. But ironically instead of providing the world with another Suleyman the Magnificent, she had blazed the trail for future generations of Harem women whose power would eclipse even her own. Ever since Suleyman the Magnificent fell for slave girl called Hürrem, things have been changing in Harem.

The women may have been enclosed but they were no longer powerless. In this world of threat and danger, they were beginning to play an active role.

Hürrem had broken the mold of the anonymous passive concubine by becoming Süleyman's confident and wife. The women who followed would build on Hürrem's power. But their power would be more as mothers than as concubines.

The murderous struggle for the succession had continued after Hürrem died in 1558. It was her son Selim who made it to the throne eight years later. His favorite Nurbanu, meaning the princess of light, would become the most powerful woman in the Harem. She was extremely well-loved and honoured by his majesty both for her great beauty and for being unusually intelligent.

100

She was the illegitimate daughter of two Venetian noble families captured by an Ottoman Admiral.

Her name was Cecilia Venier-Baffo. She was seized and brought to Istanbul in 1537 at the age of just twelve.

Nurbanu was presented to Selim the second when he was very young and still only a prince, and he fell madly in love with her.

When he went off to the provinces to learn to govern, Selim took Nurbanu with him. As a prince, he seemed to have been faithful to her.

Nurbanu was not just one more concubine. She was a privileged concubine of Selim's princely career. When he became Sultan, she came with him to Istanbul.

Like all the concubines, Nurbanu was a slave. But this was not slavery as in toiling in the plantations.

It was an honor and a wise career move to be a slave of the Sultan. For women, it meant the chance of being in the Imperial Harem which was a wonderful career. Because it was a finishing school as well as a Harem. You learned skills, you were protected from the wear and tear of daily life. And there was a possibility of becoming the Sultan's consort.

Sultan Selim was not the greatest catch for Nurbanu. He hadn't aged too well.

Selim the second was a great disappointment. He came after Sultan Süleyman, who was one of the greatest Ottoman Sultans, and Selim was called Selim the sot.

Selim was more of like his father in one respect. He loved just one concubine and even married her. But in all their years together they have had only one son, Murad. Though they did have four daughters.

The first duty of an Ottoman Sultan at all is to produce healthy heirs. So Selim had to get on with it pretty sharpish and produce more sons which he did towards the end of his reign.

With all the Princes battling to be Sultan, these new sons from other mothers would be a threat to Nurbanu's son when Selim died, which he soon did.

He came to rather an ignominious end. One can guess probably because he had been hitting the bottle. In the bathhouse, he stubbed his toe and slipped over. As Turkish baths are all stone inside, he hit his head on the stone and died instantly.

The death of a Sultan is often a crisis. Because there's that period between the death of the Sultan and the arrival of the new Sultan on the throne. If the new Sultan was not in Istanbul, that period could stretch into three to four weeks.

So there was a possibility of rebellion of a Prince trying to take over the throne. So often they would hide the fact the Sultan had died.

101

Nurbanu took control. Nurbanu hid Selim's body in the ice rooms in the palace cellars until her son Murad returned from the provinces to take his place. She only announced his death after her son arrived.

This action by Nurbanu was a remarkable one, but it was also part of the role of people at the heart of power. And from the end of the sixteenth century on, it was so often women who were there at the very heart.

So when Murad arrived from the provinces, he was obviously going to become Sultan but then he had the problem of fratricide. He has got five brothers living in the palace.

Murad spent some time alone with his mother. She reminded him of his duty to kill his brothers.

Murad spent a lot of time very unhappy thinking about it. But in the end, custom and the pressure of his mother and certainly Ottoman politics said he had no choice.

For the mothers in the Harem, there was a terrifying sense of paranoia. The state of constant anxiety.

I sometimes try to imagine myself in the place of one of those women. I am sure they raised these children knowing full well that their son might be executed.

The Ottomans took care of letting one son be successful and making him without any contenders for the throne. If one or two of his brothers survived, then there is civil war. One or two boys' death versus thousands of people being killed in a civil war is what they are talking about.

Murad made up his mind. It was a night of terror in the Harem.

The very first political act he took was to have his brothers executed. So that only one line would remain.

The first sight that the population of the capital city saw of Murad's reign was the coffins of the little princes emerging from the doors of the Palace. Although there was nothing new about Sultans' killing their brothers, this was the first time it had happened under the nose of the people of Istanbul.

One of the mothers then killed herself. She had failed in her prime function as the mother of a prince. To keep her son alive.

102

In 1574, Nurbanu was triumphant. As the mother of the new Sultan, she would now rule the roost in the Harem. She was the first woman who acquired the title of Valide Sultan. 'The Queen Mother.'

The Sultan based his policies principally on the advice of his mother. It was appearing to him that he could have no other advice as loving and loyal as her's.

She corresponded as the mother of the Sultan with Catherine de Medici and Queen Mother of France.

A Venetian ambassador wrote,
'All good and all ill come through the Queen Mother.'

She was an absolute top figure in the Harem. But she was still watching out for her son's career. Because she rose and fell with him.

There was one threat to her position. Her son had a favorite, Safiye.

It was a problem between the bride and the mother-in-law. Murad the third loved his favorite, Safiye Sultan very much. Nurbanu's jealousy and cruelty towards Safiye was something recorded in our history.

Like so many of the Sultans, Murad was going against Ottoman tradition by singling out one woman.

When he became Sultan, his job was then to produce a lot of sons. It was a kind of his insurance in case Safiye's own son should become ill and die. But he didn't. He stuck with Safiye. And this situation really troubled people.

Nurbanu tried everything to make her son meet other women and go to bed with them. She found many beautiful concubines. And she organized nights with dancing.

The gift of two concubines by his sister was a trick that turned the situation around. And off he went. So reluctant in the beginning, he had no problem.

After this, Murad almost pushed Safiye aside and began going with other women.

Against all traditions, Murad even started to sleep among the women inside the Harem. Nurbanu had him where she wanted him. In bed making more Princes.

This symbolizes that the Sultans were more restricted to the palace and in particular to the Harem. The tradition of campaigning every summer was dying away.

Nurbanu was the one who encouraged Murad the third to take up his residence in the Harem. This meant that she had more power over him than previously been the case for any woman in Ottoman history. And you can see her as a pivotal figure in increasing the role of the Harem and its head the Valide Sultan in the running of the estate.

It's about power returning from the periphery of the Empire. As it grows to return towards the center and now you go down to the center, it's the palace. And you go to the center of the palace, it's the Harem. And who's in the Harem? It's the women.

103

In Murad's reign, the Empire reached its peak. Stretching from Iran in the east, to Budapest in the West. Murad and his mother had the Harem extended, and more and more women were brought in from all over the Empire. Numbers rose from about one hundred and thirty, on Selim the second's death to six hundred on Murad the third. People then and since muttered darkly about decadence and decline.

During Murad the third's reign, the size of the Harem has increased greatly. But I can't see any reason why having a larger Harem should cause an empire to decline.

Some Ottoman Pashas disapproved the development of the Sultanate of women.

The Harem was close to power. Indeed there was a window looking onto the council chamber in the Imperial Palace where the Sultan would overhear the proceedings in the council.

Only men can become Sultans. But women are political actors. So in a sense, it means the top woman in the female hierarchy in the palace is not only a political role but it's a top political role. The palace is the seat of political life.

Nurbanu's Harem was like a department of the state within the Sultan's Palace.

The Harem was run like a large corporation. All the department heads would have novices to train. And the departments were things like the mistress of sherbet, and mistress of dressmaking, mistress of jewels, mistress of the coffee, mistress of the laundry and the general housekeeping.

In the time that Nurbanu was the Queen Mother, we really can talk about a kind of a firming up of the hierarchy of women in the Harem. At the very bottom, we've got basic servants. People who boil the water for the laundry put the coal in the furnace. This kind of service.

Then I think we need to think of it as bifurcating into a reproductive, a kind of a concubine track and in the administrative track. There's a management team in this Harem. The Chief officer of the Harem is a woman called the Harem stewardess. And she's got her own staff. She carries the keys. She's in charge of all the various service divisions within the Harem.

104

The other important Harem officials were the black eunuchs. Guardians of the sacred space. Theoretically akin to angels who unlike men could pass between heaven and earth. They were the only people who had access to both parts of the palace. They could go both into the Harem and into the male section of the palace. A black eunuch could talk to the Queen Mother about affairs of state. The Queen Mother herself couldn't then come out into the male quarters and discuss the things but the black eunuch could. In fact, it is the black eunuch who runs the Empire. They were very important people and because they were also the controllers of the Sultan's charitable trust, they could become extremely wealthy. They were on the same level as Grand Vizier in the protocol.

The palace midwives could become wealthy too. They didn't run the Empire but were central to the Harem. Midwives of the palace were very popular and they came to be very rich and they owned big houses. They were given very precious presents after they had delivered the babies.

They also advised on health and contraception. For unlike Christians at the time Muslims were allowed to use contraception.

The major method was 'coitus interruptus' which people would know as withdraw.

There was always the argument about the practice of contraception.

This was the argument between Jews and Christians. You're doing something against God and nature. Because you're not allowing the sexual act to reach its conclusion. The Muslim attitude was if God really wanted the child to be born and that child will be born.

105

Midwives in the Harem would have prepared tampons and other barriers. These would have been coated with oils, herbs, and honey. Most of the known methods were for women but there were some for men too.

Wood tar was seen as an extremely effective contraceptive when inserted into the vagina. And then it was also seen as an effective contraceptive if it is smeared on the penis.

Wood tar obviously wasn't something Murad was using. He had a lot of children. He probably wanted to have children from all the concubines he liked. More than a hundred cradles were being rocked in the Harem at the same time. In fact, the foundations of the state were swinging.

Murad had a hundred and twelve children. When he died, he had twenty seven daughters and twenty sons alive.

All the babies would be born within the Harem. The tradition was to let the pregnant woman sit on a chair and give birth to her child in a sitting position. And midwife would take it from under the chair.

You knew that even as you were giving birth, your son might become the next Sultan. But there was death too. Though someone could come and kill that child. You had to watch out him all through his life.

106

Murad was overdoing it. One son was not enough but this was too many. It would cause a crisis when he died.

People think that an Ottoman Sultan would have a large number of children with a Harem. In fact, most of the Sultans had a very limited number of children. And they took great care not to have too many children.

Safiye, the mother of Murat's first son, concentrated on building up her own political position. She also competed with his mother in choosing new slaves for him. Nurbanu must have been furious. This was her job.

The female hierarchy of the Harem was very keen on keeping control of who the Sultan slept with. Because that's how they kept control of the reproduction process. And that was their source of power. Because they were very powerful.

Within the palace, Nurbanu's power was expressed in her living quarters.

The Queen Mother had her own large apartment of almost twenty rooms. Because she was a strong woman with high status. A large number of rooms reflected that status. The Queen mothers were generally very rich too.

Because the Sultans respected them very much and gave them very valuable presents and lands.

Much of Nurbanu's money went towards mosques and other vast charitable works, including military installations. This was a statement of power on an international scale, that had up until really the time of Hurrem. It has been the prerogative of males in the dynasty. The women who succeed Hurrem, political actors are noted for their buildings.

Anybody who saw the mosque that Nurbanu and her successors built would know of the importance of the Queen Mothers. This was expressed in its stone.

Nurbanu was still at the height of her powers when she died in 1583 at the age of fifty eight. She was the first woman to be buried in the same tomb as her Sultan. She had a state funeral against all tradition. Her son, God's shadow on earth, participated.

There is a wonderful miniature of the emergence of her casket from the palace and Murad is walking in front of it.

This was very unusual. A demonstration of his attachment and the importance is given to her. When her son died twelve years later, his successor immediately executed his nineteen brothers.

107

The people of Istanbul saw nineteen coffins coming out of the palace gate. It was said that the angels in heaven wept when they saw it.

The public outcry seems to have been what put an end to the practice of Sultans' slaughtering their brothers. But in some ways, the solution would be worse for the Princes and better for the women.

From the beginning of the seventeenth century, things changed for the sons of Sultans. This would make it easier for strong women to step forward to fill the power vacuum being created. In the past, Princes have been sent off to the provinces to learn to govern. And then all but except one, had been killed when their father died. Then they were usually kept alive but they were confined within the Harem in what was known as the Kafes which means a type of cage.

Kafes in Turkish means the cage in which birds and chickens are kept. It's also the place where lions and tigers are locked. Mothers of Ottoman Princes call their sons 'Aslan', which means lion in Turkish. So when a place in the Harem was built for them to be locked up, they called it Kafes. Because Princes, like lions, were locked in there.

These were gilded beautiful apartments in the Harem where they could live for years. Just waiting. Never knowing from one day to the next what was going to happen to them. Never knowing whether their brother might be deposed and they might be pulled out and made Sultan themselves. Never knowing whether the mutes might come in with a bowstring and finish them off.

Difficulty with the cage is that the Princes were withdrawn from the day-to-day running of the Empire. So in this Kafes, a locked Prince would really know very little about politics. That may be one of the reasons why their mothers were so important in their lives. Because their mothers would know the important political situations in the Harem.

108

Kösem was the woman who used her political experience when her sons were locked in Kafes.

Kösem in Turkish means Guide. In the Ottoman Palace, her reign lasted about thirty years. She was like a female Sultan.

Kösem possibly the daughter of a Greek priest or a Bosnian girl was the favorite of Sultan Ahmet the first. She was unusual in having several sons. Once again a Sultan is adopting one woman, one concubine in this very special way of allowing her to continue to reproduce beyond just her first son.

Kösem's route to power was paved with weak Sultans. She came on the stage when they were mad or underage. Her son Murat the fourth was only twelve years old when he took the throne. Kösem was the Queen mother. She was, in reality, a regent. She wrote the most marvelous candid letters to the Grand Viziers.

She says,

'I must be driving you nuts with all my questions but on the other hand, you drive me nuts too.

You really give me a headache. But I give you an awful headache too. How many times have I asked myself? I wonder if he's getting sick of me? But what else can we do?'

You get a real sense of a political nature. The person who is engaged as a person and as a ruler. The Grand Vizier turned to Kösem when there were problems finding food for the army.

'You say attention must be paid to provisions for the campaign. If it were up to me it would have been taken care of long ago. There is no shortcoming on either my part or my son's.'

Kösem really came into her own, when her son Murad the fourth, a strong Sultan, died in 1640. He left no heir and had killed all his brothers but one. Her other son Ibrahim. Kösem had persuaded Murad not to kill Ibrahim because he was mad.

Murad died and people came to the door and said, 'Murad is dead, your Sultan.'

And he didn't believe them. He thought this was another trick of Murad.

He feared that he was going to be executed just like his other brothers who were executed by Murad. So he had to be persuaded that this was not the case and Kösem, his mother was clearly instrumental in that.

Kösem had to bring the body of Murat to convince İbrahim that Murat was dead. So İbrahim agreed to come out and be made to Sultan.

Nobody expected that Ibrahim would become the Sultan. He was known as an emotionally disturbed, and a handicapped individual.

However, Sultan Ibrahim was not mad. He had a brain tumor. He always said he had a headache and he couldn't eat. He used to say that his spelling was worsening. He was aware of himself and his sickness. When he was writing a letter, he used to start straight, then turn the paper upside down and continue to write. He generally expressed that he had a headache all the time.

Any dynasty which lasts for as long as the Ottoman Empire is sooner or later going to get a nutter on the throne. Mustafa the first was the mad Sultan, not İbrahim. The Ottomans over their whole history did very well. There were very few. But the ones happened in the mid seventeenth century.

It was the job of a Queen Mother to do anything she could to smooth over these political ruptures. One of the main job requirements is that when there is a dynastic crisis, you fix it. You smooth it over.

And Kösem did a pretty good job.

Kösem represented at least continuity. She had been in power really for longer than anyone else. And she was very careful to keep it that way. People came in and out of the Palace. No one was really building up sort of contacts and the expertise that she was.

There was nobody strong at the center of the Empire. And it seems, that is why the Queen Mothers became powerful. Because there had to be somebody to keep the work done. Given the crisis that the Empire was going through during her lifetime, we can say it was Kösem who accomplished the survival of the Empire.

The Ottomans have lost some of Murad the third's conquests in Iran and the Caucuses. The Empire was facing a rebellion in Anatolia and Istanbul and losing battles at sea. The last thing they needed was trouble at the top. But İbrahim was not just incapable, he was also impotent.

He could not be cured for a while and they were, of course, terrified that he was going to die childless that would have meant the whole country could go into a Civil War.

People were thinking that the Empire was dissolving. But the Ottomans had ways of dealing with the problem.

109

There are special books written on sexual matters and these are called Bahname. They are known as the book of love or book of lust.

In fact, Bahname is a book of medicine. But especially after the sixteenth and seventeenth centuries, it became the book of sexuality in the Ottoman Empire. Bahname, the book of classic medicine had lost its identity. It contains drugs and treatment methods in sexual diseases. There are drawings and beautiful miniatures in Bahname.

But some of these prescriptions were kept as secret. They were especially prescribed for the Sultan or the Sultan's family. Here is a very interesting prescription which was said to give such a potency to a man who used it could satisfy ten women without himself losing anything from his lust.

'You have to hunt for hundreds of large red ants and pour sesame oil on it. Leave it as exposed in the sun rays for twenty days. At the end of the twentieth day, pound them in a mortar until they become a uniform mass. It will be applied to the fingers, toes, and armpits. The potency during sexual intercourse is enhanced to an incredible degree. It will give much more pleasure.'

There are symbolic expressions in these books. Particular attention should be paid to the characters in Karagöz and Hacivat stories. 'Kirli Nigar' in the story is told as a woman. The word 'Kir' in Turkish means dirt, but also it is also used for the penis. Thus, by this method, it is explained indirectly that Nigar is actually a man.

Famous Cevdet Pasha was one of the most important scholars of the Ottoman period. He was the official historian of the state. He worked on Legal Science. He had written 'Mecelle' which is the code of civil law and also written two books, called 'Tezakir' and 'Maruzat'. In these books, he had written that they used women to make children only. They had some other entertainments.

Anyway if we get to our subject again, Bahname seems to have worked for Ibrahim.

Eventually, Kösem taking a lead in this, Ibrahim was induced to take a concubine. And with the birth of his first son, a huge collective sigh of relief came. He then goes on to become excessively interested in sex.

They say he was especially interested in fat women. Once he insisted, "Bring me the fattest woman in Istanbul!" and they found and brought her. He spent time with her for many days and all the time she told him fairy tales. Once she told him the sable story and the Sultan wanted to hear it every day. It was about a Sultan who really loved sable furs. Everywhere was decorated with fur. The chairs were fur, the curtains were fur. In order to make the story real, he wanted everything to be covered with fur.

He imposed a fur tax on the Empire. Because he wanted to line rooms in the palace with fur and mirrors. Ibrahim made his sisters come and wait on one of his concubines as a servant. I mean this was a complete perversion of the hierarchy of dignity and service and seniority. Those must have been very difficult years for Kösem. But obviously, it did not isolate her from being a political player because she still had the connections to help engineer his removal from the throne.

By the end of his reign in 1648, the Empire was weakening. The Venetian Navy was at the entrance to the Dardanelles. There was starvation in the capital city and the Viziers decided that he had to be deposed and finally his mother Kösem agreed to this.

110

Kösem wrote to the Grand Vizier,
'In the end, he will leave neither you nor me alive. We will lose control of the government. The whole society is in ruins. Have him removed from the throne immediately.'

For the sake of the Empire and her own political career, she was prepared to sacrifice her son. She had a grandson on hand to take his place.

She took his son Mehmed to the council. She didn't overestimate the Vizier's abilities.

With his six-year-old son on the throne, Ibrahim was in his prison again.

The person who was ruling the palace was Kösem Sultan. So she had to agree to her son being imprisoned and her grandson being on the throne. But Kösem could not let this continue. Ibrahim supporters might have tried to reinstate him.

A fatwa was issued by Şeyhülislam. Saying there cannot be two Sultans in one country. Officials went to the 'Kafes' with an executioner and had Ibrahim strangled.

111

With İbrahim out of the way, Kösem had a new problem. The boy Sultan's mother wanted her share of the action. Once again an older woman had a young rival jostling her for power. During the reigns of her two sons, Kösem had been the Queen Mother. Now with her grandson on the throne, she wanted to continue in power as Queen Grandmother. But her grandson had a mother, a young woman called Hatice Turhan. Now Turhan with affection around her, wanted to have the position of the Queen Mother.

There was a whole new rivalry between two Queen mothers. First time in the Ottoman Empire that there were two women at the heart of power. Two women who in a sense were acting as regents.

Kösem had to move into the palace of tears where the former Sultan's women would be sent according to traditions. But she refused to leave Topkapı Palace.

One reason Kösem might have been reluctant to remove herself from the centre of politics was that the new Sultan's mother was quite young. She might simply have felt that it wasn't the wise thing to do. But we have to remember also that she probably simply did not want to give up this densely exciting political life that she had enjoyed for so many years.

So Kösem stuck around and a deadly tug of love began with both women trying to influence the young Sultan.

These Regent Queen Mothers Kösem and then Turhan as political actors needed to communicate. And the whole question was, how could they do it? As they were in the harem, they spoke behind the curtains. They were obviously there, quite close but simply not visible. Sometimes they spoke directly. Sometimes they whispered answers through the curtains. We even heard about an incident in which young Mehmet turned to the curtain and said what answer he would give. And the answer was then conveyed to him.

Kösem defended her influence on her grandson.

Kösem,

'You said this to the Sultan. My dear, who taught you to say these things? Such patronizing behavior toward Sultan is impermissible. And what if the Sultan is instructed?'

Turhan was not so easily defeated. On the night of September the second, 1651, things came to ahead.

Kösem Sultan wanted to take her grandson from the throne and put another Prince whose mother was more malleable. That Prince was also six or eight years old.

The young mother thought that in order to save her son she should eliminate Kösem. So that night she told her guards to find and strangle her.

That was the only way she could get rid of Kösem because she wasn't going to retire voluntarily.

This is reminiscent of a couple of centuries earlier when the tension and the rivalry were among princes and brothers. Now, this kind of rivalry has displaced itself into the palace and it is among powerful women.

A eunuch spoke up for Kösem in front of the young Sultan. With the order of Turhan, they split his head with an axe immediately. His blood and brain were dashed on the rich carpet, right in front of the young Sultan. He then signed his grandmother's death warrant saying she should be strangled but neither cut with sword nor bruised with blows.

Some of the slaves hunted for Kösem. She hid in a cupboard and it was said that her presence was betrayed by her dress which was sticking out of the cupboard's door.

Seeing two great jewels at ears, slaves immediately tore them. They were two diamonds as big as chestnuts. And beneath each diamond was a ruby. Those earrings have given her by Sultan Ahmet.

She was a controversial person. She did everything for political power and she acquired great wealth. She was never satisfied.

As with her predecessors Nurbanu and Safiye, Kösem was highly praised by many people. Simply for her role as an important figure in the dynasty. I think by the time of Kösem we can say that she was revered as Queen Mother.

Kösem's young rival Turhan continued as regent for five years. But then her son and his advisers took command. As the centuries have passed, the women have continued to be criticized for meddling in politics and bringing down the Empire.

It's hard to say whether the sultanate of women was a good thing or a bad thing. They did what they could. They struggled to survive. They did what they had to do. And some amazing women emerged.

112

"I told you about the women who came to the Harem as slaves and then governed an empire in much worse conditions than you had. They didn't even have any protectors as you had."

We were alone in a small room.

"My protector? I didn't know that I had a protector. Who is my mysterious protector?"

I laughed out of anger.

"Harem is the house of special purpose. You must have already understood its purpose."

113

The House of Special Purpose

When the old woman finished her sentence, I attacked with the dagger that I hid on my leg to her throat. The woman's words had caused me to lose my consciousness. All I thought was to kill the old woman.

But then, I expected that the soldiers would fill the room and start firing. So I grabbed the woman under her chin, passed behind her, and leaned my back against the wall. Now I could see the entire room. This time I was pressing my dagger more strongly on the woman's throat.

I knew those murderers wouldn't quit to chase me. But I did not think that they could kill me through an old woman in the harem section of a palace that was no longer used.

The old woman continued to speak calmly, regardless of the dagger and my anger. "People always tell you what to do. However, the important thing is to know what you should not do. I'm not your enemy."

114

In my father's absence my mother ruled the country disastrously. Every decision that she had made brought us closer to our disaster. It was as if she was constantly shouting in the echo chamber. She had no knowledge or ability to run an empire. Now she did not have time to overcome her deficiencies.

She was German and was widely but wrongly believed to be a German spy. People believed that my mother was a traitor. She was the cause of all the troubles. She was giving my father drugs and my father was always drunk.

The truth was that my father was very exhausted. And every decision he made worked out badly. It was better perhaps to make no decision at all. My father was struggling in the swamp. Maybe it would be better if he never moved.

My father returned home from the front-line for Christmas and the New year of 1917. Every Thursday evening a small Romanian orchestra played in the red drawing-room. My mother used to sit by the fire, staring into the glowing embers. She seemed unusually sad. My father whispered anxiously, "Oh my love, why are you so sad tonight? She turned and looked at him, "Why am I sad Niki? I can't say really. I think my heart is breaking."

Even the weather made it worse. In February, 1200 locomotive engines froze and burst. Food and fuel could not be transported. In Petrograd, hunger sharpened people's anger. At this critical point, my father made a decision to leave his strife-torn capital and return to the headquarters at the front-line.

My father decided to command the army by himself, in order to close his failure in policy and prove himself to Russia and to my mother. In fact, he had escaped from the capital. Because he couldn't achieve it. He was focused on one task. Defeating the Germans. But that prevented him from noticing what was happening around him.

We began to realize that in some way my father had given up. He had somehow innerly abdicated probably some six months before the real abdication. He didn't believe in himself anymore.

115

Meanwhile, we were isolated from the capital city and my mother's main concern was that her children had measles, except me.

As he couldn't bear my mother's persistent letters, my father said he would return home. But the train was not coming.

My father had to abdicate for the train to arrive, and he did so. We did not learn of my father's abdication until the next day.

On the 2nd of March, more than three centuries of Romanov rule came to an end when my father announced his abdication. As my siblings were still ill, I was the only child who was informed about the situation. I looked as if I took it well but then I crouched in a corner, and cried. I was terrified that the revolutionaries would come to take my mother away. Almost a week later my mother told the news to my siblings.

In the Palace, both water and electricity had been cut off. Our home had given us a sign of our dark future. Our house, where we had very happy days, was no different from a dungeon. The provisional government had placed us under house arrest. Our isolation was strictly enforced. We were not allowed to leave the palace, to receive visitors, to use the telephone or the telegraph, and our letters were even checked for invisible ink.

And not only my father had been forced to abdicate but also his brother Michael had rejected the throne. Now there was no Czar at all.

Alexei called me. He asked why everyone was upset and why our mother was crying. I couldn't hide anymore.

"You know our father does not want to be the Czar anymore, Alexei."

He looked at me in astonishment, trying to read in my face what had happened. "What do you mean? Why? Who is going to be Czar then?"

"I don't know. Perhaps nobody knows."

There was silence. Then he said, "But if there isn't a Czar, who is going to rule Russia?"

By the time, my father returned home. The Alexander Palace was in the hands of the revolutionary guards. No one was present when my father met my mother, except us. We were waiting at the door and trying to listen and see them.

My father sank into my mother's arms and wept.

116

While my father was going out into the garden, he was wearing an old uniform from which he removed all the epaulets and rank marks. He was shoveling the snow away from the footpath every day. He never gave up wearing his old coat which was all stained. It was not even clean. But he went to the garden every day without getting tired and continued to work like a simple worker.

They shaved our hair because of measles. The soldiers were looking at us and laughing. The best response to their taunts and humiliation was to have fun. We were smiling and joking with each other when we left our rooms.

Especially Anastasia was never leaving my father alone. She thought that the soldiers could harm my father. If she was nearby him, she could protect my father.

When we returned to our rooms, we were making plans for how we could get rid of this captivity. We turned it into a game. Alexei was becoming the Czar, we were his generals. We were defeating the treacherous revolutionaries and Russia was free.

One day we have heard that the new provisional government requested and received asylum in Great Britain for us. My father did not want to leave Russia, and especially the capital city. But he said it was a good idea for our security. But my mother wanted revenge.

The English King, George the 5th was the cousin of both my father and my mother. But obviously, he was unprepared for the public outcry. Because the British, like the Bolsheviks, thought that my mother was a German spy, but she was more English than anything else.

My father finally convinced my mother. My mom and we were going to England. My father would stay in Russia and fight to get back his throne. My mother accepted, albeit reluctantly, but she required us to recover from measles. She said that we could not bear the bad conditions of the journey, especially Alexei.

We were still making preparations as if we were going to England. However, one day, I heard that my father's cousin withdrew the invitation to asylum. At one dinner, my father said, "We will go to Crimea and grow flowers."

117

As the sun rose on the first day of August the moment came for us to leave. Kerensky said we could go. We drank our last cup of tea and left Tsarskoye Selo at 6.10 o'clock in the morning. Thank God. We were all safe and together.

After almost five months under house arrest, we left the Alexander Palace for the last time. At the Alexandrovski station we boarded a special train. Its final destination was unknown. At the stations we had to shut our window curtains that nobody should see us. They did not want anyone to see us.

We played guessing games along the way. We were asking each other about the types of trees, the names of the places we passed. We mostly made up. The most ridiculous answer was winning. We were laughing and having a lot of fun. Maybe we had applied this way to forget what we had experienced and to escape from our sorrows.

The journey into exile was long and slow. Four days in a train, two more on a paddle steamer. On the evening of the 20th of August, we finally reached Tobolsk. My father had once visited this house twenty-five years ago. And it was renamed as freedom house since the revolution.

We examined everything in the house from bottom to attic. It was dirty and smelly. There was almost no furniture at all.

Many rooms had an unattractive view. Then we went to the garden. It was nasty. My father complained about the plumbing and overflowing. toilets.

By mid-december the temperature dropped below minus 20. We tried to keep busy ourselves by chopping woods and pulling Alexei around on his sledge.

We used to gaze out of the window. We were waving people on the street. But we were invisible to them. None of them had heard or seen us. We were playing games to guess their names, what they did, how old they were. Of course, these were the questions that we would never learn their answers.

118

By the late fall of 1917, we heard that Lenin and his Bolsheviks were poised to seize power. On the 7th of November, the Bolsheviks headed for the Winter Palace, which was the stronghold of Kerensky's seven-month-old government. The provisional government was destroyed. But the damage to the Palace consisted of chipped paintwork and a broken window.

Kerensky managed to flee Petrograd. He would never return. Lenin and the Bolsheviks were now the rulers of Russia. In one stroke of the pen, he conceded great tracts of the Russian Empire's Western Borderlands nearly half a million square miles and more than one-third of the population.

My father eventually heard of the disintegration of his Russia. That was the first time that my father was really regretted his abdication.

We spent more than six months as prisoners in Tobolsk. New harsher guards had taken over. We were secretly sewing our bodices with our last pieces of jewelry.

My mother was knitting stockings for Alexei. My father's trousers were torn. Our under linen were all in rags. We were allowed no walks except in front of the house, inside the high fence. But at least we had fresh air and we were grateful for anything.

Alexei was nearly 14 years old. He suffered another serious bout of hemophilia. He would never walk again. He was frightfully thin and yellow. I sat with him all day. One day he said to my mother, "Mama, I would like to die. I am not afraid of death but I am so afraid of what they will do to us here."

On the last days of February 1918, we had to cut down substantially on our expenses for food and servants. Because we couldn't afford to support all of them who were staying with us in Tobolsk.

The Bolsheviks held demonstrations almost every day in front of our new house. They were insulting my father and us. The guards inside the house were looking at us and laughing. Their behavior particularly annoyed my mother, but there was nothing we could do.

119

Lenin sent an experienced revolutionary, Vasily Yakovlev, to take my father to Moscow. He was going to face a possible trial. My father refused to go to Moscow.

My father said, "Me? Where? I will not go!"

Yakovlev said, "As Alexei is ill, you are the only one who is obliged to depart straight away."

Then my mother said, "I've noticed that they have been trying to separate me from Nicholas recently. I'm not staying here. I'm coming too."

I went with my mother and father to Moscow to ensure that my mother would not be alone if they arrested my father. Olga, Tatiana, Anastasia, and Alexei stayed in Tobolsk.

But on its way to the capital city our train was diverted to Ekaterinburg by the fiercely revolutionary Ural Soviet. There was an armed brigade which was brought specially to intimidate us. We were frightened. Although I tried not to show my feelings to my mom and dad, I thought we had come to the end of the road.

They took us to a house owned by the merchant Ipatiev, referred to as the house of special purpose by the bolsheviks. We were assigned four large rooms. A very high wooden fence was built around the house. Only the cross above the belfry was visible from the rooms. According to what I learned from one of the guards that I became an intimate friend, there was a machine gun just below the cross in the belfry, pointing at our window. There were thirteen men with rifles, revolvers, and bombs. Opposite to our window in a house on the other side of the street, there was a detachment of fifty men.

The guards were controlled by a sinister group of men who were stationed at the American Hotel, near the house. Bolsheviks had assembled there to decide our fate.

It was no longer a house arrest. It was much more like a prison.

In Tobolsk, at least we had been able to watch the world go by from our windows. But in Ekaterinburg, even that small freedom was gone. We were living in semi-darkness. We had not dared to draw the curtains. The white painted windows were too horrible.

I realized that the only way we could get out of here depended on our friendship with some guards. I managed to be friends with a few of them. One of the guards I was closest to was Ivan Skorokhodov. If I could make our friendship a little more intimate, I was sure that he could get us out of here.

120

On the 23rd of May, we were reunited again. Alexei, Olga, Tatiana, and Anastasia were brought from Tobolsk. Alexei was ill. The sailor Nagorny was looking after him.

On the 26th of May, Alexei's pain continued. A dark gentleman came whom we identified him as a doctor.

On the 27th of May, Nagorny was taken away for questioning.

On the 29th of May, there was no information about Nagorny. We thought that he might have been killed. Everyone around us was disappearing one by one.

Our staff was getting tiny. Dr. Botkin, Anna Demidova, a maid. Alexei Trop, the footman. Ivan Kurtinova, the cook and a young kitchen boy.

On my 19th birthday, Ivan brought a cake for me. But unfortunately, this was the last day I saw him. He knew how dangerous it was, but he did it anyway.

On the 27th of June, we spent an uneasy night. We kept vigil, fully dressed. Because we received two letters that were telling us to prepare to be abducted by some loyal people. But nothing had happened.

On the 13th of July, Alexei took his first bath since Tobolsk. His knee was improving. We had no news from the outside.

On Monday the 15th of July, four local girls came to wash the floors. We were very happy to see the girls. For the first time in a long period, we were able to see people other than the guards. I really wanted to talk to them, but I was afraid that the guards would get angry and punish the girls because of me.

Finally, I gathered my courage and went over to talk to them. But the guards took me away immediately. At that moment, I could sacrifice many things to be in place of those girls.

On the 16th of July, Alexei had a slight cold. We had been sawing diamonds and precious stones into our bodices for the promised liberation which never came.

On the same day, suddenly the young kitchen boy was fetched to go and see his uncle and flew off. We wondered if it was true.

Only a few days earlier, Nagorny had disappeared for questioning and he didn't reappear. We were afraid that the child would have the same fate.

121

"I know who you are," she said. "Your companion, your friend, your protector had a grandmother. Did he never speak to you of his grandmother?"

I was staggered by her words. How could she know me? Even my closest friend Gülnihal had no idea who I was. I stepped backwards and dropped the dagger.

She immediately proceeded to devote her closest attention to her important duty. She leaned over and asked for help to remove the floor. Underneath the floor, there was an extremely beautiful wooden box with pearls on it. She unlocked it and gave me the book which was hidden in the box.

"It's time. Take this book and deliver it into Rua's hands. He is waiting for you," she said and gave me a pouch which was full of gold coins.

"What do you want from me? You want me to deliver a book to a gentleman I know nothing of?"

"Ayşe Sultan, who was the mother of Sultan Süleyman, was the daughter of Mengli Giray Khan. He was the Khan of Crimea. Ayşe Sultan wasn't an ordinary concubine. She was a noblewoman who came to marry Sultan Selim the first.

Rua is a member of the Crimean Dynasty, a descendant of Genghis Khan. He attempted everything to save you and your family. If Sultan İbrahim did not have a child, his reign would have passed to the Crimean Dynasty. Even today, they have many spies in this palace as in Russia."

122

Paris, 26 June 2017

Adige closed the diary. She remembered her father telling the days how her grandmother had survived the massacre with her brother, and her brother's death on the road and their arrival to Istanbul, the attack that she faced at Pasha's house.

Pasha handed Maria to Harem after the attack and promised her that he would take her back after everything has settled down. But on her first day, her grandmother was tried to be killed by two concubines in the Harem. A man in a military uniform with German Iron Cross saved her life.

Leaving her brother's grave behind, saddened Maria most. She couldn't remain quiet at every night.

She used to say, "I didn't get you out of there, my angel. I couldn't help you meet with your most loved ones. Forgive me, brother."

Two years before her death, she went on a two-week vacation. She never cried after her arrival. She said nothing when asked but an attentive observer would have noticed his lips curl with a nice smile.

123

At noon, Adige realized that she was late for the café in the Latin Quarter and she started frantically preparing.

She was a waitress in a café despite the fact that she had inherited a huge sum from her family and lived in a rather large house in Paris. Because of her family's situation, she didn't have any close friends. After losing both her parents at a young age, she had no one in her life.

There were only two elderly retired Professors whom she trusted in life and enjoyed speaking. She was happy to see them again like every Monday, but today it would be different because it was her grandmother's birthday.

She asked James to talk about the philosophers. Her grandmother always said that Pre-Socratic philosophers saved her life.

James said, "Don't tell Albert. We cannot get rid of his mocking language. I will start talking about this topic as if I chose it by chance."

Her grandmother always told people that she had survived with the help of Sultan Mehmet the second and the Pre-Socratic philosophers. Since the books in the unique library of Sultan Mehmet the second were not very valuable for the other Sultans, many of the books were lost and some of them were sent to Harem's library. Maria met this library with the recommendation of her best friend Gülnihal and her perspective on life had changed after reading books about Pre-Ssocratics.

Adige glanced at the notes that she wrote about the five Renaissance philosophers that her grandmother loved most, before leaving home for the café.

Beneath the Crescent

Maria Romanov After 17 July 1918

Maria Romanov After 17 July 1918

Maria Romanov After 17 July 1918

Hasan

124

Topkapı Palace, 11 October 1922

I was paralyzed. I was losing my mind. I even forgot where I was. What was that book? Who was the owner? Who was waiting for me? The questions were listed one after another in my mind.

The old woman said, "Everything you need to know is in that book."

Then she lifted the carpet from the wall behind her. There was a hidden door. She pointed the door and said, "Follow the right side on the road. It will end in the Hippodrome. You're on your own after that."

I said, "I can't go. Why would I trust you? How do I know that you're not lying to me?"

"Rua is waiting for you. Don't worry, your brother will be safe," she said.

I understood that the woman knew a lot more than I thought. I said, "Gülnihal. I need to let her know."

She said I didn't have time. In response to my insistence, she asked a young concubine to call Gülnihal.

I even forgot my pregnancy for a moment with the excitement of seeing Rua. As I was hesitant to tell the woman about my pregnancy, she touched my belly with her hand and said, "If you want him to have a home and life, you should go. The Sultan and his family will leave soon. Nobody will think of you. You know, the Prince is married. His wife will not let you and your baby live."

When Gülnihal arrived I told her what had happened and asked her if she wanted to come with me. She stared at me for a long time. She was thinking about the answer. The old woman broke the silence.

"If you want to survive, go immediately."

125

As we moved through the tunnel Gülnihal said, "I knew that you were not an ordinary concubine. You lied to me."

But she didn't look like she was angry. She agreed to come by saying that she would rather die as a free woman than live as a slave.

"I had to keep my secret. I'm going to tell you everything when we get to a safe place," I said.

When we reached the door at the end of the tunnel, we hesitated to open it. The woman said the tunnel was leading to hippodrome, but it was scary not to know what was waiting for us behind the door.

"How stupid we are. We didn't take anything with us. All the money I have saved so far remained in the Harem," said Gülnihal and became angry at herself and me.

I showed the pouch that the old woman gave me to Gülnihal and said, "I have enough money for both of us. Calm down. We will succeed. We have to succeed."

We gathered all our courage and opened the door slowly. A corridor, covered with white marble was laying in front of us.

The corridor was one of the hidden paths under the Hagia Sophia. At the end of it, there was a door which was opening to the old Grand Palace, which was under the Blue Mosque. We learned that there was another Istanbul beneath the Istanbul we knew. We lived in those tunnels for a week, believing that Hagia Sophia, who has been protecting everyone for centuries, would protect us too.

I have engraved the names of my family members on the walls of the little room we stayed beneath Hagia Sophia.

We couldn't believe what we saw when we first opened the book that the old woman gave us to deliver to Rua. From the earliest times until today there was a list of all Kings and their descendants. All the kings, including Solomon, Moses, Jesus, and Mohammad. It was very clear that if anyone saw this book, he could do anything to have it.

Among the pages of the book, there was a map that would lead us to Rua. We tried to find the safest way for a long time. During the day we went out to the train station and harbor, tried to find a way to get us to the Greek side.

There were soldiers everywhere. A ceasefire was signed, but still many places were under the control of foreign troops. It was not safe to walk on the roads and ask questions as two women. Our hopes were starting to fade.

126

That evening with Gulnihal sitting in the underground room of our palace, we heard shoutings and footsteps. When we gathered not to be caught and headed towards the tunnels on the Hagia Sophia side, we came face to face with two soldiers.

The younger one pointed his gun at us. He yelled at us to lay down on the floor in the Russian language. The other one looked very carefully at my face without ever moving and without saying anything. They had the Russian White Army uniforms on them.

The soldier stared at my face for a long time without speaking and then told the other soldier forcefully to drop the gun.

He said, "Back off!"

Then he bowed respectfully and saluted. We did not know how to react with Gülnihal.

The lieutenant, like many other white army officers, was one of the soldiers who escaped from the Soviet regime and fled to Istanbul. He was tired of the English arrogant practices and joined Turks to support their war of independence. From these tunnels, they were carrying weapons to the boats waiting to be taken to the troops in Anatolia.

The lieutenant, assigned the sergeant to take us to Venice. And the next night, three of us were secretly boarded on one of the freight wagons of the Simplon Express. Although we had to go somewhere else we told them that we had to go to Venice. We believed that we could handle it after by ourselves.

There were no identity documents with us. It was years of war, and if we got caught, there was no need to be a prophet to know what would happen to us. Nobody even Gülnihal knew about the jewelry that was covered with leather on my neck and wrists. But the book in my bag and especially the money pouch could easily be found.

127

That morning, I woke up with a gun pointed at my face at a short distance. The sergeant asked me to be quiet and give him my necklaces and money pouch. Years later, I was facing the same scene.

With the scream of Gülnihal who was sleeping next to me, the sergeant turned and fired his gun. From that moment on, my eyes blackened. I jumped on the sergeant. Soon after we fell to the ground and Gülnihal hit the Sergeant's head with an iron bar. I tried to strangle him at the same time. Blood was flowing from the head of the sergeant to the wagon floor. It started to cover the whole place. I came back to life by the sound of Gülnihal's falling to the ground. I ran to her. She was bleeding from the right side of her abdomen.

We covered her wound. When the train slowed down near Mestre, we jumped off the train. I wanted to take Gülnihal to the hospital as soon as possible. She said, "Leave me behind. I don't have the strength to take another step. Just tell me who you are. I want to know the person whom I die for."

My only friend in life was dying. My parents, my sisters, I lost them all. And now Gülnihal. It's like everyone I touched was dying.

"I'm going to tell you everything if you hold on and help me take you to the hospital. But first, you must hold on," I said.

She smiled. "Whoever you are, you're my friend. Don't give up."

Then, her head fell to the right side.

I started yelling, "Don't give up. Don't leave me alone. Stay with me."

But Gülnihal had already gone. She was my only companion in the Harem, my friend, the person who saved my life many times. I laid beside her. At that moment I wanted to dive into endless sleep right there.

After a while, when I came to myself, I started looking for a safe place which was suitable to bury Gülnihal.

I buried Gülnihal under a large tree. In order to find the tree when I came back, I have engraved the letters G and M to the tree's body. I wasn't sure where my mother, father and my sister's graves were. Their places could have been changed. I wasn't sure about the fate of my brother's grave also. And now Gülnihal. I began to walk away and pray that her tomb would not be destroyed. Actually, I should have been in the place of Gülnihal.

128

Gülnihal came to Harem when she was thirteen years old. She had read almost all of the books in Harem's library. If she was born in another time and place, she could have had a very different life. But she had worked in the laundry of Harem in her whole life. As I moved farther from there, her voice was in my ears.

"Don't forget, Maria. Istanbul is the capital of the world. We may be happy about leaving Istanbul now. But we may regret it in the future. Do you remember the milestone I have shown you on the Hippodrome? Istanbul is the city where everything started."

"Every war is actually between Hector and Achilles. The golden man is the new Hector of the Turks. But Achilles will come soon."

"Remember, Maria. Every war ends in between women's legs. The Ottoman Sultans would not have married. There is a tradition of the abduction of the King's wives in Asia. That's why none of them have been married until the last years, except Suleyman Khan."

"The old Ionians had no Gods and no books delivered from the sky. They had to understand life and nature by themselves. The only weapon they had was their mind to survive. We have to use our minds. Nature gives us all the answers."

"In all religions, people are said to be equal. Am I equal with the Sultan? If I steal an apple, they cut my hand. Kings, Sultans cause thousands of deaths with their decisions, but they do not receive any punishment."

"I understand that the only crime in life is to get caught."

When Gülnihal lay down in the harem's bathhouse, she looked at the perforated dome and prayed that an angel would come down to save her. Maybe the angel she was waiting for loved her so much and took her.

129

There were Ottoman gold coins in my pouch, necklaces on my neck and diamonds and other precious stones on my wrist. All of this increased my fears. I wasn't afraid of death. I was afraid of losing my hope.

I didn't even know where I was walking. After a long walk, I came to a market place. I stood in front of a market stall selling various bread and desserts. I was carrying a fortune on me, but I didn't have enough money to buy a piece of bread.

An old saleswoman standing behind the counter approached me. She gave me a small piece of bread. I tried to refuse gently. The woman insisted. I ate the piece of bread that she had given. I realized how hungry I was at that moment. She took me to the back of the counter.

I could barely understand her words. I knew she wanted to help me with her hand gestures. I was in a mess. My hands were covered with mud. She helped me to wash my hands and face by pouring water. Then she gave me an apron and asked to stand next to her.

I knew what she wanted to do, but I couldn't decide if I wanted to stand there. Together with the old woman, I sold bread until the evening. I arranged the counter.

At the end of the day, I helped her to collect her counter and load it into a carriage. She told me to wait there and she left. She came back with two mugs of coffee and a piece of cake in her hand. She gave me money. The money should have been the equivalent of my work that day.

We sat down to drink our coffee and eat our cakes. I expected her to ask a lot of questions, but she didn't talk. In the end, I asked her in an English-Russian language.

"In the North. In the region of Tyrol. There is a church under the crescent. Near the Cold Lake. I have to go there. How can I go?"

I wasn't sure if she understood. She got up and talked to the other marketers around. She didn't like the answers she got and she just vaguely disappeared. After a while, she came back with a man.

The man looked at me carefully. He asked in Russian where I wanted to go. I don't know whether I should be happy or scared. I didn't answer his question in the first place. But then I asked the same question that I had asked the old woman in Russian while he was about to leave. He asked me again and I told him the same things. He looked at the other people.

Apparently, no one knew about the church under the crescent. The whole market tried to solve this puzzle and started talking about the church. This situation started to scare me. I thought I should get away without attracting more attention. There were no documents of my identity. What was weird that nobody even asked my name.

When I was going to thank the old woman and those around her, the Russian-speaking man came up to me with another woman.

The woman said, "The church under the crescent should be in Moena. They say that a Turkish soldier lived there a long time ago. If you're looking for a crescent, you should go there."

Then a heated debate began among the crowd. I asked the Russian-speaking man what they were discussing about. He said that they were talking about how I should get there.

130

They took me to a lorry. The lorry belonged to a family who came to the city to shop. They were going to a town called Cortina d'Ampezzo. I met the family with the help of the Russian-speaking man. I was going to travel with the children on the back of the lorry which was covered with a tarpaulin. If the road conditions would be appropriate, they would take me to Moena. Of course, if I pay my fee.

I was traveling with two little girls, who were five and seven years old. Even in those circumstances, they were quite pleased with their conditions. Even though we didn't understand each other, we were playing little games.

After a while, my eyes began to close from exhaustion. I pulled my legs around my stomach, leaned my head against the sack stack behind me and closed my eyes. My family came to my mind. Sometimes I was afraid of forgetting their faces. One by one, I thought them all. I hugged them. I kissed them.

My father used to tell me that he never wanted to be a Czar. He talked about that he always wanted to live a simple life in the Crimea in a small house with a garden.

They used to say the same things, for the last Ottoman Sultan Vahdettin, in Harem. He wanted to live a quiet life in his mansion in Çengelköy.

He said, "I sat on the toilet, not on the throne."

It was said that his daughters cried on the day of the throne ceremony. The eunuch of the Harem warned them that their tears would bring bad luck. I thought that they were similar in their fate.

Will they kill Sultan Vahdeddin and his family too? I wondered why the old woman in the Harem was so insistent on my escape. Did Rua save me one more time? If Rua was following me so closely, he should know that I was pregnant. Would he love me as I was?

131

I was thinking about the Ottoman Prince on our way to Moena. Is he thinking of me now? Does he ever wonder about me? Years after our first encounter, he called me into his room. I didn't know what to do there. While the other concubines prepared me for submission to him, I was warned how I should behave in his room.

I had two thoughts in my mind. Either I had to kill myself or him. I would never let him touch me. When we arrived at the door of his room, my heart seemed to stop beating. I couldn't breathe. This was not the excitement of the first night. I've never been closer to a man before. I have never been touched before.

I looked at the motifs on both sides of the door. Gülnihal had told me about them many times. Although the motifs on both wings were symmetrical, they were, in fact, the reflection of each other in the mirror. Those on the left side represented life and death on the right side. There was this metaphor all over the palace. I thought it was exactly the way I felt. Only one person would survive in this room.

The door of the room opened from the inside. I was frozen. I felt like they were trying to push me to get inside. But my feet were nailed to the ground. I almost fell into the room with a strong push from my back. When I heard the door was closing, my whole body was shaking.

After that, the only thing I remember was the time the Prince said, "You may leave."

In addition to all this, the worst moment that I felt was when Prince had sent gifts to my room. That was the time when I could die.

132

It was a cold morning when the lorry stopped. I thought we were stopping for another break. When the lorry's canvas was removed, the girls' father pointed to the ground with his hand, "Moena, Moena."

I gave him an Ottoman Gold, which I had previously taken from my money pouch. He examined it with a grinning face. He gave it back to me. I showed her wife's bracelet and said that it was Gold. He took the coin again and he started to bite the coin between his teeth. When he was satisfied with the payment, we said goodbye to each other.

Moena was a mountain village in the middle of the mountainous region, similar to the Siberian forests. There was a river strongly flowing in the middle of the village. The scenery was great, but I was cold. Wondering how to find the church, I began to walk towards the houses. I saw a "Turkish Street" sign.

I thought if there was a crescent, it could be here. When I entered the street I saw a fountain made of stone and a bust of Turkish military turban near this fountain. Wooden busts of a man with this Ottoman turban were found in front of the houses. It was cold and there were no people on the street. A man from the carpenter workshop of this street came towards me. He said something in Italian, but I didn't understand.

Then he started to speak in German. He asked whom I was looking for. I asked about the church under the crescent.

"There is a cold lake," I said.

He laughed. "There must be a church under the cross," he said.

"Of course if it is really a church," he added.

He must have pitied on me because he had invited me to his shop. He asked if I wanted to eat something.

133

I asked about the man whose busts were everywhere in the village.

"Hasan," he said. "Janissary Hasan. During the second siege of Vienna, he was in contradiction with his commanders. He was sentenced to death. He was able to get rid of them during the execution."

I thought how similar our stories were.

"He came here with wounds on his body. The foresters found him and brought him here, to the village. In those days lords were coming and collecting money from the peasants and confiscating their products. Hasan didn't admit this and he taught the villagers how to make guns and how to fight. The following year, the peasant demonstrated resistance to Lords' troops and the soldiers had to retreat. After that day, they did not visit this village again. The people of Moena also convinced Hasan not to go, whom they loved a lot. He got married here and had children."

After he finished his words, he took another sip of his coffee. Then he suddenly got serious.

"Your church should be in Termeno. As Lords didn't stop here to collect money because of Hasan, it was said that they hung the Turkish symbol everywhere in their village. I've never been there, I didn't see it, but it should be."

He asked, "What will you do if you find the church?"

I told him that my brother was in the white army and he ran away to this region. I said that I was trying to find him. He seemed like he didn't believe me, but he didn't insist on it.

I was so tired of being hopeful and frustrated every time. When I first came here, I was very excited to see Rua, but now I was very disappointed. Even though I wanted to reach Rua, I was afraid of my pregnancy. What would happen if he didn't want me?

"Why don't you come and get me?" I asked desperately.

134

It was evening. lights were coming from the village houses. I had nowhere to go. For the first time desolation was so painful. That moment I would have sacrificed everything to be with my family in one of those warm houses.

After accepting the man's offer, I spent the night in their house, in the little room at the entrance. Although his wife wasn't happy with my presence at first, then we became good friends and she showed me great hospitality.

I've hardly slept all night. I was very nervous. I wanted the sun to rise as soon as possible. But then I fell asleep.

I woke up in the morning with a knocking on the door. The man wasn't at home. I had breakfast with his wife and three children. We were talking in German. At the end of the breakfast, the man came.

"I found you a truck," he said. "They're waiting for you."

It was a truck carrying tree stumps. I sat down beside the logs behind the truck. At the end of a winding and long road, a small town appeared. Although I couldn't see the lake, this should be that town. After a while, the truck stopped and the driver came to the rear and said, "We came to Termeno."

Termeno or as the locals called it Tramin, was located close to the top of a mountain. The town was laying under my feet. There was a lake on the outskirts of the mountain, but I didn't know if that was the lake I was looking for. And there was the church on my left. I examined the top of the church carefully for a while. There was no sign of a crescent. I entered the church and I didn't know what was waiting for me.

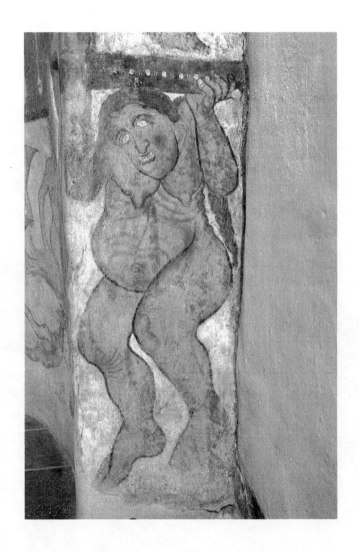

Maria Romanov After 17 July 1918

Maria Romanov After 17 July 1918

135

The St. James Church in Kastelaz

The church was decorated with a Romanesque fresco cycle showing imaginative hybrid creatures of man and animal, including creatures with dog heads, bird or fish parts, and centaurs, mixed creatures of man and horse, from Greek mythology.

I had seen in the fresco that the conflict between good and evil, day and night, sin and goodness, black and white were explained. I couldn't make sense of how the symbols in a Catholic church were so similar to the symbols in the palace of the Islamic Caliph.

The source should be single. Was this source the only God, or was it nature and the universe that we were living in, as the Presocratics had said?

I got out of the church as I lost all my hopes that I would find Rua. I walked to the back of the church. I was standing on a rock at the foot of the hillock above the town in which Tramin ended beyond the point, and my left-hand side was stretched out towards the lake.

The high hills of the other mountains ahead were crowned with forests, whose tops were then empurpled with light. Tramin stretched on either side as far as the eye could reach. The beautiful panorama was laying in front of me for a distance of eternity.

The whole world was under my feet. I was so tired and exhausted. While looking at the railroad, I thought I had seen a star with a crescent similar to the one on the Ottoman flag, on the church in the middle of the town. I thought I was losing my mind. I just sat on the rock and closed my eyes. I didn't know how long I stayed there.

136

When I opened my eyes again, the weather was getting dark. I was so cold, tired and hungry. When I looked at the church below, I saw that the crescent and the star were still there. You've come all this way, Maria, I said to myself, and tried to find a way to go down the hill with the last effort.

Then a secret instinct warned me for a moment. I had come here for a man that I saw only for a moment in my life. Maybe his name wasn't even real.

I looked around me. The valley in front of me was full of vineyards and apple trees. It was very quiet. Even its emptiness was suspicious. I remembered my good old days with my family. I couldn't even imagine these days. How death, separation, and grief were at that time away from us.

137

Is the curse of Rasputin still following me? Will this curse never come to an end? The man whom everyone thought was a healer and a priest was a man who used to get some kind of drug from the cannabis plant as ancient pagans did. It was actually a miracle plant. This plant could be used as a healer in the right hands, or it could turn into a lethal weapon in the hands of Rasputin. Thanks to the oils obtained from this herb, he even managed to make women become slaves to him. How on earth did he fool my poor mother? He convinced my mother that he could heal my brother and he had mystical powers.

I remembered the frescoes of the church.

The frescoes reminded me of the paintings on the walls of the houses where we were held captive. Red Army soldiers, painted disgusting pictures of my mother, father, and sisters. We were desperate.

Everything must have dignity.

Some people were asking among themselves, how this strong man could allow himself and his family to be struck like that and not demand satisfaction for such insults.

138

I was descending the slope of the hill to the church with crescent and star symbols. It was a very steep slope. My feet were barely carrying me. Along the way, I saw the same symbols on the walls of the houses. They were like guiding signs to follow. I couldn't understand why there were Ottoman flag signs in a village in the south of Austria.

I came to the town square. There were several stores underneath the adjacent buildings. I saw that there were only crescents on some of the buildings this time. I felt like I was in a small village in Istanbul, not in Europe.

At last, late in the day, and half dead with fatigue, I reached the entrance of the church, which was situated at the base of the town.

I went into the church garden. The gate was closed. I didn't dare to go inside. I was also very tired. Right across the door, there was a big old stone. I sat on it, rested my feet and waited for my breath to return to normal. When I took off my shoes, the wooden door with two wings was opened. An old man appeared at the door. He seemed blind. After turning his head from left to right, he stepped slowly towards me. He still wasn't looking at me. I held his hands that reached out to me. He bowed.

"Welcome home, princess," he said.

"Thank you," I said.

I had no idea what to say and what to do.

"Wait here please," he said and returned to the church.

I was just looking around and waiting.

After a while, two young girls came out. They said the same things and greeted me in a very respectful way. We went into the church and went upstairs to a room.

They said we were going to Rua together. I was so surprised that I didn't ask any question. I was following their instructions. I was just doing what they said.

139

First I had a hot bath. Then I put on some clothes that they brought to me. When I left the bathroom, I saw a beautiful dining table waiting in the middle of the room.

For a minute, I forgot where I left my bag. Or was the cause of all this hospitality to steal the contents of my bag? Did they know what was inside? I remembered that I took my bag with me to the bathroom.

When I walked into the bathroom again, I was relieved to see that it was standing in the corner. I opened each page of the book separately, hoping that the steam didn't harm it.

The content of the book was incredible. Page after page was filled with the genealogies of the kings, their birth and death days, places of their birth and their tombs. The whole world could enter a war with one another for this book. I seized it and rapidly turned over its pages, and my emaciated finger fixed itself on one of them.

I closed the book and stared at the wall for a while.

"What about my family?"

Even Alexei's burial place, along with my mother, father, and sisters, was recorded correctly. I was very curious about who kept these records. Because only me, Pasha, and a few servants of Pasha knew Alexei's grave.

There was no one in the room except me. When I left the room after examining the book, I saw two girls waiting outside the door. It was just like in the Harem. We went downstairs together. Nobody was talking. There was an absolute silence of death around. A deep silence fell into the church. This silence, which appeared so long to me, only proved one thing. It was time to leave.

We got out of the church. I understood that we were headed towards the lakeside.

For a long time, we walked through the houses on a straight path. At the end of the houses, we entered the vineyards which I admired. After a while, we turned left and started to climb up the slope.

We turned right and started to walk through another vineyard. There was a house in front of us.

"Is he there?" I asked.

The girls nodded.

At last, we reached the house. "You can go in," said the girls.

"You?" I asked.

"We were just told that we should accompany you along the way," they said.

Now my heart was beating very fast. Who was there? What was I going to face?

I pushed the door. It was open. It was a two-story wooden house. When I entered, an old woman greeted me. After saluting, she accompanied me to the upstairs and pointed to the room across the stairs.

I opened the door slightly. I saw a man lying on the bed in the corner. I opened it a little further, and when I entered, I saw that the man in the bed was Rua. His eyes were closed. I was so scared if he was dead. I came closer and I saw him breathing. He should be sleeping. He must be sleeping.

140

"Rua. I came," I said, hesitatingly.

He was giving no sign of life. Only his chest was moving as he was breathing.

Actually, I was delighted, to be left alone without his maids. There was complete silence. I closed the door. Like I always imagined, there were only two of us in the world now. I lied down next to him. I closed my eyes thinking that I was in the most peaceful place I could be.

141

Rua was very sick. He could barely breathe and he could hardly walk. With the thought that it might be good for him, we took long walks at the vineyards and chatted for many days.

We were talking neither about the past nor about the future. I think we both were aware of the moment. Rua didn't have much time. For me, the nightmare was continuing. I kept losing one by one whoever I loved.

That day Rua said he wanted to take a walk by the lakeside. The distance was too long so I insisted on going there with a car and then to walk along the lakeside. He didn't accept it. So we started to walk by giving frequent breaks on the road, together with one of the maids.

"I heard you," said Rua. "Everybody already knew what would happen. Only your father didn't understand the severity of the situation. Or maybe he understood, but he couldn't get out of the trap that had been set up because he had no preparation before."

Rua's words reminded me of those days. I knew I was about to find out the reasons for the disasters that we had been through.

"If you don't know your house, someone who knows it better than you, will come and take it away from you. As you know, with the Great War, four Empires have been lost in history. Ottoman Empire, Austria - Hungary Empire, German Empire, and the Russian Empire. It was normal for the Ottoman and Austria - Hungary Empires to lose their countries because they were on the losing side. But the Russian Empire was on the winning side. While the dynasty members of the other two Empires were sent into exile, your family was killed until your last member."

I wondered if our relatives shared the same fate after us.

"Russia was the new Troy. The British Empire was disturbed by a powerful empire in the east. But because they were allies with the Russians, they could not do it themselves. They found the German Kaiser, who was in love with your mother. As a natural consequence, he hated your father. The German Kaiser found the best shooter that he could find. He was Vladimir Ilyich Lenin. Alexander Ulyanov who was Lenin's brother was executed for attempting the assassination of Czar Alexander III."

I didn't believe what I heard. It was like he was telling the lives of others, not mine. How can this be true? The British King George the fifth was my father's cousin, just like the German Kaiser Wilhelm the second.

As I went through all this, Rua continued to tell.

"Wilhelm asked Lenin to kill only your father and to send your mother and your siblings to Germany. At first, Lenin was convinced. Then he decided that Wilhelm was planning to claim rights in the throne of the Russian Empire through you. Then he decided not to leave any of the heirs behind. His cousins betrayed your father. But if there is a betrayal, the important thing is that whose fault it is. The one who betrayed or the one who was betrayed. For example, why had Mongolian emperor Genghis Khan never been betrayed?"

142

I could not say anything. "So my father is responsible for all of this?" I could only ask.

Rua continued to tell instead of answering my question.

"Genghis Khan had a very well-functioning intelligence organization. Knowledge is the greatest power. You know, Maria. You were born as a princess. Then you became a slave. You will decide what happens next."

"Can't we decide together?" I asked desperately. I thought that he didn't want me because of my pregnancy.

In the meantime, I didn't realize that we reached the cold lake. Rua sat down near a small plane tree.

"I don't have much time left."

A deep silence fell on all around. The lately roaring winds were hushed into a dead calm; nature seemed to breathe no more, and was sinking into the stillness of death.

He continued, "I planted this tree on the day when I heard that you had survived. It succeeded. So you can do it too. The whole world thinks that you're dead. If you show up, your past won't let you go. It's much easier to live as a dead living being than a living dead. When I die, make me buried under this tree. I will be the soil. You will be the rain."

I didn't know what I had to worry about. Betrayal of my father's cousins or Rua's disease. After all those years I finally reunited with Rua and now, he is talking about death.

"You know that I'm a successor also. But I cannot be the Scourge of God. Because I don't believe in God," he said with a smile. "You don't have to follow in the footsteps of your ancestors."

When we got home, we heard loud voices coming from the upstairs.

"Can't we find a way?" asked someone.

"I can't hide the whole Russian Empire in my backyard," the other one replied.

Rua wanted me to wait downstairs and then he went upstairs. I couldn't hear what they were talking about. I heard a door opening. I approached the stairs with the hope that I could hear something.

"I am no longer Khan's son. You are Rua's father from now on."

143

We sat in the garden without talking for a long time. Then Rua turned to me and said, "Sometimes the safest place in a forest fire is in the middle of the fire. Just as you were safe in the Harem of the Ottoman Empire that you had been fighting for centuries."

Then, the man that I saw next to Rua in the ballroom approached. The guy's name was Arche. He was Rua's brother.

Rua started talking before Arche.

"I knew that my father would send an executioner. I'm honored by his choice."

"You know the rules as much as I do, brother," Arche said.

"She's pregnant."

"I know."

He turned to me and said, "Stay in the middle of the fire. Nobody can hurt you here."

I remained silent for a while. I was terribly shocked by what I had seen and heard. My heart was deeply touched by the thought that he was at the point of death.

Then he turned to Arche and said, "I demand a quick death. An honorable death."

I couldn't believe what I heard. I can only remember that I was screaming and pushing Arche. Then I fainted.

144

When I opened my eyes, Rua was looking at me with smiling eyes.

"You're not dead? Did they forgive you?" I asked with excitement.

"I have no intention of dying before I see you and your baby are safe," he replied.

Arche couldn't do it. According to traditions, he had to stand behind Rua and kill him with a dagger by striking his heart.

When he went to the back of Rua, he put the dagger on the floor and walked away. I never heard from Arche after that day.

The next morning I woke up with the news of Rua's death. Did someone else complete the work Arche hadn't done? Or was he died because of his disease? Even today, I still do not know. I told his father he wanted to be buried under the plane tree. He only nodded without even looking.

On that rainy day, we buried Rua where he would take his endless sleep. I could not leave him for a long time. My hands fell under the ground with the rain. The last person I loved was gone. Rua took too much risk for me to survive. My baby and I should deserve his loving-kindness.

Rua's father left me the house in Tramin. Two of the maids stayed with me to help me during my pregnancy and birth.

For a long time, I couldn't decide whether these women were trying to help me or to kill me after birth.

145

Termeno / Tramin, 26 June 1923

Today, my precious, beautiful son was born. I named him Otmar. I registered Rua as his father. Although some people see him as the heir of the two empires, he is just my little boy. I just want him to have a blissful, peaceful and tranquil life.

I think of Rua every time. I thank God that he has given me such a gallant protector, a friend, a lover, so generous and wise. I knew that I was safe with him, under his protection.

146

Tyrol, May 1918

There were two guards at the door of the house in the large garden, overlooking the Caldaro lake. It was the late hours of the night. The man, who hid his face with a large piece of fabric, was 150 meters away from the house. He checked around for the last time and he started walking towards the house.

One of the guards saw the wolf-embossed medallion which the man took out from the inner pocket of his jacket, went inside and told the man to wait. Soon after, the door was reopened and the messenger was taken to a small shack in the garden of the house.

"Wait here. Rua will be here soon."

When the visitor left, Rua entered the house and saw his father in front of him.

"Don't get involved," Khan said. Although his speaking tone was very calm, he was very furious. "You will be killed," he continued. While Rua was thinking about what to say, his father continued, "I should never have sent you to Romania."

"They're going to kill the Imperial family. We can rescue them. There are many men who we know among the Bolsheviks."

"Does the holy German Emperor ask for help from an exiled prince? Have you lost your mind?"

"It's our home. We can help. At least we can help the innocent children."

"Our family was also innocent. You want me to help people who has descended us from the throne and our family members became enemies to each other. If you try to do something without my permission, I will kill you with my own hands!"

147

Ipatiev House, Ekaterinburg, 17 July 1918

The Czar turned to the commandant and stammered, "What? What?"

The firing began and lasted two or three minutes. The Czar was killed instantly followed by Czarina and the servants. Sisters and the heir were still alive. Something had made the bullets ricochet and fly around the room.

When the executioners saw that the girls did not die, they thought that a divine power was protecting them.

The executioners went over to the girls lying on the floor writhing from pain and started taking off their clothes. When they undressed the girls and the heir, they discovered that they had been wearing garments full of jewels that had not been pierced by the bullets.

The executioners have forgotten their duties and started collecting precious stones. The commandant who was very pissed off about this situation fired his gun and shot on the ceiling.

"If you don't want me to kill you before the White Army arrives, leave the jewels in your hands immediately and load the bodies all into the truck."

148

The truck moved out of Ekaterinburg in the early hours of the morning. The corpses were on it. It stopped after going ten miles.

Only the driver was left next to the truck, and others were gathered at the mine where they would bury the bodies.

When the driver attempted to open the door, the man approaching him from his backside, closed his mouth with his hand and cut his throat.

Meanwhile, another man jumped to the back of the truck to see if anyone was alive.

149

Three men spurred their horses to their utmost speed. The forest was preventing the gallop of the horses. But it was also hindering the view of the soldiers.

They hastened into the forest, followed by some of the executioners, who were firing after the three men. But they rapidly increased the distance between them, and found themselves beyond the reach of the bullets.

"Too far, you fools!" bawled the commandant. And, as he spoke, he aimed at one of the horsemen who was farthest to the front, and fired. He watched their disappearance.

Meanwhile, in the forest, the other three men with Maria and the heir were riding their horses in the other direction.

150

At sunrise, they reached the carriage which was waiting for them in the forest. The man who was standing by the carriage was blind. As every blind man, he could see the sounds. He had heard the horsemen approaching before they showed up.

"Is there a place where we can eat?"

"The back of the car is available and you can find there as much food as you want."

Gibraltar handed the blind man a pouch of gold. The man proceeded quietly and disappeared into the forest.

Three horsemen carried the two mortally wounded bodies to the closed section behind the carriage. When the men took off the clothes of the wounded girl and boy, what they saw became even more terrible. They were bathed in blood.

"If we can't get to the doctor in time, both will die. We have to be quick."

151

"You said one person," the host said, when he saw the people entering and carrying the wounded young girl and boy. He was not happy with the situation.

"I want twice as much money."

"Shut up! Otherwise, you won't have time to spend that money. Where is the doctor?"

"He is inside"

Gibraltar, who did not like the attitudes of the peasant, decided to silence him forever before leaving the house.

After examining the injured girl and boy for a while, the doctor recognized who they were. As tears flowing down his cheeks, he asked, "Sooner or later, everyone was expecting this sad end. Any other survivors?"

"Unfortunately not," Gibraltar replied.

From that moment on, the doctor continued to treat them as if he was worshiping.

"The heir's condition is too bad. He must lie down for a long time without moving."

"This is not possible. We will hit the road tonight."

"He would die on the road, before he goes a few miles. In this state, it would be a murder to take him on a journey."

"It would be a murder to leave them here. They will surely go after them to finish the work that has begun. We have to go."

While going out with the injured girl and boy, the peasant came near to Gibraltar. Gibraltar reminded Isaac of what to do with a head sign. Upon the doctor's insistence, they took him with them and placed the injured girl and boy in the carriage. After the doctor got on, they started to wait. Soon Isaac also came in with quick steps and got into the carriage.

"Where are we going?" asked the doctor curiously. "The less you know, the better," replied Gibraltar.

152

They traveled to the Crimean Peninsula at the end of their journey, which lasted much longer than it should be, since they mostly set off at night and stayed too much to rest the injured passengers. The doctor expressed his discomfort with being in Crimea.

"None of us are safe here. Why did we come here?" he asked.

"Crimea is our home. There is no safer place in the world for us."

Indicating that he did not like this answer at all, the doctor said that he had to go to the city center to find the medical supplies he needed in the treatment of the injured girl and boy.

"Isaac will go with you. We will leave tonight. Isaac knows where we will be."

"It would be great," the doctor replied.

After Isaac and the doctor left, Gibraltar told David to drive the carriage towards the dock. After hiding the horse-drawn carriage at the dock of Sevastopol, Gibraltar left the shift to David and went to the back of the vehicle next to the injured girl and boy. They were both lying without showing any signs of life. He did not know what to decide about the doctor. As long as he was with them, there was no problem, but he still bothered to go on this journey with someone they didn't know who he was.

As the sky darkened, Isaac and the doctor arrived. The two big bags that the doctor carried were caught the attention of Gibraltar, but he did not say anything. "Welcome. Let's eat. When it gets dark, we will hit the road. The captain will be waiting for us on the boat called 'Tatar' with a black hull."

153

When the clock passed midnight, they took action. They stopped in front of the boat named 'Tatar' on the quay with the horse carriage.

"Isaac, go ahead with the doctor. Come and let us know when the doctor sets up a suitable place for the injured girl and boy," said Gibraltar.

The captain greeted Isaac and the doctor at the stern of the ship and led them towards the cabins. After ten minutes, Captain and Isaac came to the carriage and the vehicle quickly moved away.

David was spying on the boat, hiding in a far corner of the dock, where he could see the boat. He soon saw that a group of fifty soldiers had begun to board the boat. He quickly moved away from there.

"I told him this was our home," said Gibraltar, after hearing what David had said.

No boats were allowed to leave the harbor that night. The soldiers searched all boats in the harbor and all the houses around.

Later in the next night, a small fishing boat began to sail away from the shore and sail towards the black sea.

"The last two teardrops of the Russian Empire have fallen," said Gibraltar, thinking of the siblings' departure from their homeland.

When they were on their way to Istanbul sailing in a small fishing boat in the Black Sea, the Heir's sick body could not resist this difficult journey any longer.

Maria, who was already trying to cling to life with difficulty, believed that she had no reason to live anymore after the Heir's death. She attempted suicide many times.

One of the men who helped their escape, said, "Death doesn't welcome you yet. And also Rua is waiting for you."

154

Hagia Sophia, Istanbul, 26 June 2017

Adige arrived at Sultanahmet Square at midnight. It was a beautiful summer night. The square was still very crowded. Adige was sitting in a cafe close to Hagia Sophia to spend time.

At 02:00 am, the streets were almost empty. She walked through the door of the old Hippodrome on Nakilbent Street. After a long walk in the dark with a little flashlight, she reached the great hall. She started reading the writings on the wall.

"Nobility passes through blood, not by law", OTMA

She continued to walk in underground tunnels, looking at the sketch which her grandmother drawn in her diary.

She was walking in the opposite direction that her grandmother had followed about hundred years ago. She stopped when she found the gate of the harem to the hippodrome. She tried to open it. She hoped the room behind the door was empty.

The door was locked. But it wasn't too hard for Adige to open it. Because it was an old door. She was standing in the room where her grandmother, Gülnihal and the old concubine were standing about 100 years ago. She began to walk around the room.

She wrote the names Maria and Otmar on the last page of the Ottoman dynasty family tree which she copied from the book that her grandmother took with her.

Maria and Gülnihal had taken a photograph before they left Istanbul. She put that photograph, the family tree list, and the jewels which the prince gave to her grandmother years ago into the wooden box with pearls on it.

She placed it underneath the floor where it was 100 years ago, with a note saying, By the lost Şehzade.

155

Moscow, November 1918

The German General was waiting for Lenin in the room at the headquarters of the revolutionaries. With his expressionless face and almost motionless body, he was almost looking like one of the furnitures in the room. Soon Lenin entered the room. He shook his guest's hand and sat down at his desk after saluting.

"Good to see you again, General," said Lenin.

"You too."

"I hope I didn't make you wait too long. Can I offer you a drink?"

"Thank you. I do not have much time. You must be busy too. Our Emperor demands the delivery of the Empress and the children."

"Your Emperor did not act honestly. We all know that he was the one who spreaded the news that I was a German spy. Sorry I can't deliver the family."

The general's facial expression changed for the first time since he had entered the room. With his gaze, he made clear that he was disgusted with the man in front of him. "Without our help, you would already be a dead man. You should thank God that I'm not a bandit like you, I'm a German soldier. Otherwise, your previous words would be your last words."

Even though Lenin was furious with General's words, he was trying not to show his anger to him. "Thank you for your support. I agree with you, especially you had helped very much personally. However, the conditions have changed. I have to do the right thing for my people."

"You can be sure that our Emperor will not leave this behavior unpunished. Also, will you still be able to sit in that seat, when your people find out who you are collaborating with?"

"As I just said, General, the conditions have changed a lot. I think your Emperor should start thinking about his own fate, instead of thinking about punishing me," said Lenin.

"You'd better prepare a farewell speech to the people you love so much," said General and he quickly left the room without saluting.

156

A Few Weeks Later

Seeing the man sent by the banker, Lenin started to speak in a reproachful voice, "I would like to host Baron personally. Doesn't he think of coming to my visit?"

"You know how things work," the man replied.

"Of course," he said and he offered his guest a glass of vodka and continued his words. "I hope the Baron liked the gifts that I had sent him."

"Yes. He asked me to thank you for your meticulous work. However, he is wondering why the donation to the foundation is delayed."

"I'm sorry, but unfortunately there is no one left who can donate anymore. Please convey my sadness to Baron. And we both know that the Baron doesn't have to worry. Who can get the assets in the banks unless Baron wants?"

The banker's representative understood that there was no other topic to talk about anymore. Before he left, he could not refrain from saying a few words that would bother the arrogant man in front of him for a long time.

"You must know that the Baron will never be happy with your words."

"Baron must also know that Soviet Russia is a government that cannot be disciplined by the constant threat of the throne," Lenin replied.

"I understand you, but your men have already lied to you. Two of the children have survived," said the man and left the room.

157

Topkapı Palace

During the restoration work in the past years, an ornate wooden box was found under the floors of the Harem section of the Topkapı Palace.

When the curator of the museum took the box to his room and opened it, he encountered a small notepaper. By the lost Şehzade

He thought that the museum staff was making a bad joke. Other than this note, there were forty-one pieces of jewelry, the list of the Ottoman Dynasty genealogy, a photograph, and a few sheets of paper in the box.

The curator, who was also a professor of history, was more interested in the photograph and notes than jewelry.

In the photo, the two women posed standing side by side in front of the Sirkeci train station. Behind the photograph, the name Gülnihal was written with old Turkish letters. Although he examined it for a long time, he could not recognize the two women in the photo.

Then he began to study the notes. There were different dates and place names at the top of each page. There were several pages in Russian handwriting that seemed to have been removed from a diary. There was no clue on the papers about who had written the notes. The curator, who was also a member of a family that emigrated from the Crimea to Turkey could not believe his eyes when he read the notes. He was sure that someone was making a bad joke.

When he got up from his desk and walked out of his room, he couldn't see anyone around.

After he finished reading the notes from the diary, he looked at the faces of women in the photo again to see if it could be real.

Although he knew the faces of almost all members of the Romanov dynasty, he turned on his computer on his desk to be sure. He examined the pictures of the Czar Nicholas' daughters, one by one.

He asked himself, "Could it be real?" Then his friend who was an expert in precious stones came to his mind.

158

"Yes, my friend, these jewels are all real. I can even assure you that you can't find similar pieces anywhere. These are very well preserved, unique pieces," said the friend of the museum curator.

The curator, who wondered whether the jewelry was original or not, only to find out the authenticity of other documents, turned his attention back to the notes from the diary and genealogy list.

He had never heard of the name which was at the end of the list before. There were Şehzades who were not recorded in the genealogy list before, but their names were known by everyone. Also, the name on the list was not one of the names given to the Şehzades.

The curator examined the documents that came out of the box for a long time and took photos of the jewels with his friend. Then he sent the jewels to the archive of the museum. He took the notes from the diary, genealogy list, and the photograph with him and went to his home.

About the Author

Haluk Çay was born in 1976 in Istanbul. After graduating from the Faculty of Law of the University of Istanbul. He started his law firm in Istanbul in 2003. He has been working as a Lawyer especially, in customs and smuggling, taxes, international trade, and transport laws. He spent many years researching the history of law, science, philosophy and wrote numerous articles. He is happily married to Dr. Tuğçe ÇAY and has a son Demir Efe ÇAY.